AF538946

RURAL WOMEN ENTREPRENEURSHIP

RURAL WOMEN ENTREPRENEURSHIP

Edited by

Dr. S. Maria John
Dr. R. Jeyabalan
Dr. S. Krishnamurthy

First Published - 2004

Reprinted - 2017

ISBN: 978-81-7141-889-3

Rural Women Entrepreneurship

Published by:

DISCOVERY PUBLISHING HOUSE PVT. LTD.
4383/4B, Ansari Road, Darya Ganj
New Delhi-110 002 (India)
Phone: +91-11-23279245, 43596064-65
Fax: +91-11-23253475
E-mail: discoverypublishinghouse@gmail.com
sales@discoverypublishinggroup.com
web: www.discoverypublishinggroup.com

Printed at:
Infinity Imaging Systems
Delhi

Preface

The Post Graduate Department of Commerce, Cardamom Planters Association College, Bodinayakanur 625 513 (Tamil Nadu) organized a two-day National Level Seminar titled "*Entrepreneurism in Rural Economy*". In the seminar, many eminent personalities, Professors of various universities and college and research scholars have presented their research articles and papers on matters relating with financial and social constraints of women entrepreneurs, opportunities for women entrepreneurs, development through co-operatives and Self Help Groups. Sincere and modest efforts had been taken in the present book by the co-editors viz Dr. R. Jeyabalan and Dr. S. Krishnamurthy, Readers in Commerce, Cardamom Planters' Association College, Bodinayakanur to select quality oriented research articles and the same are presented under the title "*Rural Women Entrepreneurship*".

The research articles presented in this book provide maximum possible information useful regarding the subject matter taken up for discussion. This book also set out to provide its readers the global aspects of entrepreneurism. The perspectives of co-operative entrepreneurism also take a vital part.

We are happy to express our sincere thanks to the honourable management of CPA College, Bodi, the contributors, the participants on the seminar and all our colleagues who supported it on bringing this task to a great success. Our earnest thanks are also due to Mr. Tilak Wasan the Proprietor, DPH Publishers and Booksellers, New Delhi for the sincere efforts taken in publishing this book.

Dr. S. Maria John
Dr. R. Jeyabalan
Dr. S. Krishnamurthy

Contents

List of Contributors

Dr. V. Gopalakrishnan, Reader and Head, Department of Commerce, Aditanar College of Arts and Science, Tiruchendur 628 216.

R. Prakash Babu, UG Professor of Commerce, AVVM Sri Pushpam College, Poondi-613 503.

Sr. Josephine Nirmala, Reader in Commerce, Fatima College, Madurai-1, Tamil Nadu.

V. Sathuragiri, Lecturer C.P.A. College, Bodinaykanur. Tamil Nadu.

Dr. S. Maria John, Reader in Commerce, CPA College, (Madurai Kamaraj University), Research Advisor and Supervisor, (Manonmanium Sundaranar University), Bodi-625 513.

Mrs. A. Mary Grace, Lecturer (SG) History, JA College for Women, Periyakulam.

Mrs. V. Kavitha, M.Com., M. Phil. (Lecturer in Commerce).

R. Anitha, M.Com., PGDCA., (Lecturer in Commerce), Vidyasagar College of Arts and Science, Udumalpet-642126.

M. Padmini, III B.Com, Nadar Saraswathi College of Arts and Science, Theni.

Haji Dr. M. Sheik Mohamed, M.Com., M. Phil., Ph.D. FICWA, PGDCA, FMSPI, PGDFM, Reader and Head, Department of Commerce, Jamal Mohamed College, Bharathidasan University, Tiruchirappalli-620 020. Tamil Nadu.

N. Arul Prakash, M.Com., Full-Time M. Phil. Scholar, Jamal Mohamed College, Tiruchirappalli-620 020.

Dr. S. Eswaramoorthi, Reader, P.G. Department of Commerce, C.P.A. College, Bodi-625 513.

Mrs. J. Jayalatha, M.Com., M. Phil., Ph.D. Research Scholar, Department of Commerce, Nallamuthu Gounder Mahalingam College, Pollachi-642 001.

Dr. K. Ramamoorthy, Professor of Commerce, Department of Commerce, M.K. University, Madurai-21.

Mr. S. Ramesh Kumar, Research Scholar, Department of Commerce, M.K. University, Madurai-21.

Dr. Punithavathy Pandian, Professor, Department of Commerce, Madurai Kamaraj University, Madurai-21.

R. Eswaran, Ph. D. Research Scholar, Department of Commerce, Madurai Kamaraj University, Madurai.

A. Lakshmi, Research Scholar, Department of Commerce, St. Joseph's College, Trichy-2.

Dr. R.M. Nagammai, Lecturer SG, Lady Doak College, Madurai.

Dr. V. Madasamy, M.Com., M. Phil., Ph.D, Reader in Commerce, Ayya Nadar Janaki Ammal College, Sivakasi-626 124.

G. Thangapandi, M.Com., M. Phil. Research Scholar, (F.T), Ayya Nadar Janaki Ammal College, Sivakasi-626 124.

Dr. M. Inbalakshmi, Senior Lecturer in Commerce, G.T.N. Arts College, Dindigul.

Dr. G. Anjaneya Swamy, Director, Centre for Entrepreneurship Training and Development, Pondicherry University.

Deepak Raajan, Research Scholar, School of Management, Pondicherry University.

A. Jayarani, M.Com., M. Phil., Ph.D., Research Scholar, Department of Commerce, Madurai Kamaraj University, Palkalainagar, Madurai-21. Lecturer in BBM Department, Salem Sowdeswari College, Self Financing Courses Wing, Kondalampatty, Salem-10.

Dr. S. Murugesan, M.Com. M. Phil. Ph.D., Head and Reader in Commerce, P.M.T. College, Melaneelithanallur.

Dr. C. Azhakappan, Lecturer (SG) in Commerce, Thiruvalluvar College, Papanasam.

Dr. S. Krishnamurthy, M.Com, M.Phil, Ph.D., Reader in Commerce, C.P.A. College, Bodinayakanur-625 513.

S. Balamurugan, Lecturer in Commerce, C.P.A. College, Bodinayakanur.

Dr. V.M. Selvaraj, M.Com., M.Phil., Ph.D., AICWA., B.Ed., Reader in Commerce, AKGS Arts College, Srivaikuntam-628 619.

Miss. S. Jeyarani, M.A. M.Phil., Lecturer, Department of Economics, The American College, Madurai-2.

Dr. M. Dhanabalan, M.Com., M.Phil., Ph.D., Lecturer (PT), Department of Commerce, MKU College, Madurai-2.

S. Kamaraju, Lecturer in Commerce (S.G.), P.G. and Research Department of Commerce, A.V.V.M. Sri Pushpam College (Autonomous), Poondi-613 503, Tamil Nadu, India.

S. Raju, M.Com., M. Phil., Lecturer in Commerce, A.V.V.M. Sri Pushpam College [Autonomous], Poondi, Thanjavur-613 503.

Dr. K. Sivaloganathan, Reader in Commerce, Kanchi Mamunivar Centre for Post-graduate Studies, Pondicherry-605 008.

Dr. V. Madasamy, M.Com., M. Phil., Ph.D., Reader in Commerce, Ayya Nadar Janaki Ammal College, Sivakasi-626 124.

S. Senthil Sreenivasan, Lecturer, P.G. Department of Corporate Secretaryship, Bharathidasan Government College for Women, Pondicherry-3.

Haji Dr. M. Sheik Mohamed, M.Com., M. Phil., Ph.D., FICWA, PGDCA, FMSPI, PGDFM, Reader and Head, Department of Commerce, Jamal Mohamed College, Bharathidasan University, Tiruchirappalli-620 020. Tamil Nadu.

N. Arul Prakash, M.Com., Full-Time M. Phil. Scholar, Jamal Mohamed College, Tiruchirappalli-620 020.

R. Jegadeeswaran, Lecturer in Economics, M.K.U. Evening College, Theni.

S. Jothi Mani, II M.Com., N. S. College, Theni-625 531 Tamil Nadu.

Dr. Samwel Kakuko Lopoyetum, Senior Post-Doctoral Research Fellow (PDRF), Department of Cooperation, Faculty of Rural Social Science, Gandhigram Rural University, Gandhigram–624 302, Dindigul District, Tamil Nadu State, India.

Mr. A. Lourdu Arockiaraj, II M.A. Cooperative Management Student, Gandhigram Rural Institute, Gandhigram-624 302.

Dr. S. Kannan, M.Com., D.G.T. Ph.D., Reader in Commerce, Kamaraj College, Tuticorin.

A. Padrakali, M.Com., M. Phil., S.G., Lecturer in Commerce, A.P.C. Mahalakshmi College, Tuticorin.

Mrs. M. Malathy, Lecturer, Department of Commerce N.S. College Theni 625 531, Tamil Nadu.

Dr. S. Ganesan, Faculty of Commerce, Madurai Kamaraj University College, Madurai-625 002.

Prof. C. Eugine Franco, SG Lecturer in Commerce, St. Xavier's College (Autonomous), Palayamkottai 627 002.

Sivagami, Faculty in the Department of Commerce APAC for Women, Palani, Tamil Nadu.

Mrs. M. Pushpa, Faculty in the Department of Commerce APAC for Women, Palani, Tamil Nadu.

Mr. P. Sorubarani, Faculty in the Department of Commerce APAC for Women, Palani, Tamil Nadu.

Vennila Fathima Rani, S., M. Phil., Scholar (Commerce), St. Joseph's College (Autonomous), Trichirappalli.

Dr. S. Michael John Peter, Reader, Department of Economics, Arul Anandar College, Karumathur, Madurai-Dt 625 514.

V. Sarvanan, Research Scholar, Department of Economics, Arul Anandar College, Karumathur, Madurai-Dt 625 514.

M. Manimaran, II M. Com., C.P.A. College, Bodinayakanur.

K. Ramasamy, II M.Com., C.P.A. College, Bodinayakanur.

Nalini, III B.Com., AC College for Women Cumbum, Tamil Nadu.

Financial and Social Constraints of Rural Women Entrepreneurs

Dr. V. Gopalakrishnan

In India, the female population is 495 million as per the census in 2001 contributing to nearly half of the country's population. In traditional societies, women are confined within four walls of the house performing mainly household activities. They are regarded as the better half of the society. It is also true that "behind the success of every man, there is a woman". In reality, women contribute a lot to the success of men but they are not recognised properly. In the male dominated social setup, women get very poor recognition which in no way match to their achievements. In addition, their resources and potentials are not fully utilised.

The socio-economic development of a country cannot be fully realised so long as its women are confined to subordinate position and their talents remain unexplored. Women entrepreneurship is becoming a reality now-a-day due to pull and push factors. Between the pull and push factors, the former takes it as a real challenge with an urge to do something new and take up an independent occupation. The other category of women establishes business enterprises to overcome the financial problems of self and family. Over the years, the phenomenon of women entrepreneurs is largely confined only to metropolitan cities and big towns in India.

In order to achieve the objective of social justice, it is necessary to harness the latent skills and potentials of women, especially the rural women. They play a key role for rapid and sustained economic development of the rural areas and the ultimate prosperity and development of the nation.

Though the Central and State Governments have launched many entrepreneurial development programmes especially for women, there is no remarkable achievement in rural areas. In Tiruchendur, the population of women outnumbers the population of men but women are not emerging as entrepreneurs due to various constraints. Therefore, an attempt has been made to identify the constraints of rural women entrepreneurs and to take suitable remedial measures to overcome their problems.

Area of Study

The study is conducted in Tiruchendur, which is the second of the six abodes of Lord Muruga. It is situated on the east coastal line at the southern end of India. It is sixty kilometres away from Tiruneveli on the eastern side and forty kilometres away from Tuticorin on the southern side.

Objective

The objective of the study is to highlight the major financial and social constraints encountered by women entrepreneurs in Tiruchendur.

Methodology

The study is mainly based on primary data collected from women entrepreneurs in Tiruchendur through an interview schedule. It is an empirical study based on survey method. In Tiruchendur, women entrepreneurs are emerging in various fields namely Tailoring and Garment manufacture, Handicrafts, Beauty Parlour, Palm Gur manufacture, Catering Services, Dairy Farming, Job Works (Typing, Xerox, Lamination, etc.) and the like. Since most of the women entrepreneurs are running small-scale organisations, the data regarding the number of women entrepreneurs are not available in the government departments. Hence 40 women entrepreneurs are selected by simple random sampling technique and the data are collected during January 2003.

A list of financial and social constraints encountered by women entrepreneurs is identified and a pre-test has been conducted. In the light of the experience gained from the pre-test, the list is finalised and the sample respondents are asked to rank their constraints. In order to analyse the data, Garrett's ranking technique is adopted and the following Garrett's formula is used.

Garrett's Formula

$$\text{Per cent Position} = \frac{100\,(R_{ij}-0.5)}{N_j}$$

Where, Rij= Rank given for the ith variable by the jth respondent;

Nj= Number of variables ranked by the jth respondent.

By using this formula, the result obtained is compared with Garrett's ranking table and scores are appended. The total scores for each item are added and ranks are given according to its total value.

Findings and Discussions

Financial Constraints

Finance is the lifeblood of any enterprise. It has to be available at the right time in right quantity. ·Availability of adequate financial support accelerates the success of an enterprise. If an entrepreneur is unable to mobilise the needed finance, her dream will not come true. The women entrepreneurs are facing various financial constraints in mobilising finance. The ranks given by the respondents to the ten financial constraints encountered by them are exhibited in the Table 1.1.

By using Garrett's formula, total scores for each item are calculated and ranks are given according to its total value and the results are presented in Table 1.2.

Table 1.1. Financial Constraints of Women Entrepreneurs

Rank / Constraints	Number of Respondents										Total Respondents
	I	II	III	IV	V	VI	VII	VIII	IX	X	
Shortage of Fixed Capital	16	5	5	4	3	2	2	1	1	1	40
Shortage of Working Capital	3	5	5	5	5	4	4	3	2	4	40
Negative Attitude of Banks	4	3	5	5	4	3	4	6	2	4	40
Delay in Sanctioning of Loan	4	7	6	3	4	3	3	4	5	1	40
Inadequate Size of Loan	3	4	4	6	3	4	5	5	4	2	40
Inability to offer Collateral Security	5	8	6	5	3	4	3	3	1	2	40
Rigid Repayment Schedule	2	4	2	2	5	6	6	5	5	3	40
Ignorance of Banking Procedure	1	1	2	1	4	5	4	6	9	7	40
Bureaucracy & Red-tapism in Government Departments	2	3	4	6	6	5	4	3	3	4	40
Lack of Accounting Skills	0	0	1	3	3	4	5	4	8	12	40

Table 1.2. Financial Constraints of Women Entrepreneurs

Sl. No.	Constraints	Total Score	Mean Score	Garrett's Rank
1	Shortage of Fixed Capital	2606	65.15	I
2	Shortage of Working Capital	2047	51.18	IV
3	Negative Attitude of Banks	1997	49.93	VI
4	Delay in Sanctioning of Loan	2145	53.63	III
5	Inadequate Size of Loan	2003	50.08	V
6	Inability to offer Collateral Security	2271	56.78	II
7	Rigid Repayment Schedule	1855	46.38	VIII
8	Ignorance of Banking Procedure	1548	38.70	IX
9	Bureaucracy & Red-tapism in Government Departments	1948	48.70	VII
10	Lack of Accounting Skills	1370	34.25	X

It could be inferred from the table 1.2, that shortage of fixed capital is the serious financial constraint of women entrepreneurs followed by inability to offer collateral security, delay in sanctioning of loan, shortage of working capital and the like.

The study reveals that shortage of fixed capital is the vital constraint of women entrepreneurs. They need huge amount in the form of fixed capital to float an enterprise by investing in fixed assets. The respondents reveal that they have to entirely depend upon their family members not only for fixed capital but also for seed money to get loan from bank.

The second important constraint is the inability of women entrepreneurs to offer collateral security. The sample respondents state that properties of the family are in the name of male members and are not able to offer the collateral security. Further, the delay in sanctioning the loan and inadequacy of loan also block the success of women entrepreneurs.

The respondents view that the banks have a negative attitude towards women entrepreneurs because the banks consider them as "mobile" citizens who follow their husbands whenever they get transferred. They view that unmarried women may settle with their husbands in some other place after their marriage. Therefore, bank authorities have a suspicion about the survival of the enterprise.

Generally, there is a belief that women do not know banking procedure and are lacking in accounting skills. But it is interesting to note that the study has revealed that most of the women entrepreneurs are competent enough in banking procedures and they do not lack in accounting skills.

Social Constraints

The combination of the words "women" and "entrepreneur" seems to be socially odd in India, especially in the rural context. Apart from the problems common to all entrepreneurs, women also encounter various social problems. The ranks given by the respondents to the ten social constraints encountered by them are exhibited in the table 1.3.

Table 1.3. Social Constraints of Women Entrepreneurs

Rank / Constraints	Number of Respondents										Total Respondents
	I	II	III	IV	V	VI	VII	VIII	IX	X	
Lack of Self-Confidence	1	1	2	3	3	5	4	4	6	11	40
Absence of Family Encouragement	3	7	5	4	4	3	4	4	4	2	40
Prejudice against Women	7	8	4	6	5	3	3	2	1	1	40
No Risk-bearing Capacity	1	2	2	3	4	4	6	7	7	4	40
Dual Role of Women	12	5	5	4	6	3	2	1	1	1	40
Male Domination	6	5	6	5	4	4	3	4	2	1	40
Lack of Exposure	1	1	3	4	4	6	7	6	7	1	40
Problems in Public Relations	4	4	5	6	3	4	4	5	1	4	40
Lack of Economic Freedom	5	6	6	3	4	3	4	3	4	2	40
Fear of Social Security	0	1	2	2	3	5	3	4	7	13	40

By using Garrett's formula, total scores for each item are calculated and ranks are given according to the total value and the results are presented in Table 1.4.

Table 1.4. Social Constraints of Women Entrepreneurs

Sl. No.	Constraints	Total Score	Mean Score	Garrett's Rank
1	Lack of Self-Confidence	1523	38.08	IX
2	Absence of Family Encouragement	2089	52.23	V
3	Prejudice against Women	2367	59.18	II
4	No Risk-bearing Capacity	1693	43.33	VIII
5	Dual Role of Women	2485	62.13	I
6	Male Domination	2241	56.03	III
7	Lack of Exposure	1789	44.73	VII
8	Problems in Public Relations	2054	51.35	VI
9	Lack of Economic Freedom	2151	53.78	IV
10	Fear of Social Sęcurity	1408	35.20	X

Table 1.4 shows that dual role of women is the major constraint of women entrepreneurs followed by prejudice against women, male domination, lack of economic freedom, absence of family encouragement and the like.

The study has revealed that the dual role played by women entrepreneurs is the severest of the social constraints. Women assume too many roles in a family. She has to be a loving mother for her children and a housewife to the rest of the family. The long cherished role of mother and housewife hampers her to devote full time and efforts for her entrepreneur role.

The second important constraint is prejudice against women. The respondents felt that they are not recognised properly and are never considered capable of executing an enterprise successfully. The respondents viewed that the serious barrier to women entrepreneurs is the persistence of the belief held by both men and women that entrepreneurship is a male domain. Further, male members interfere into the day-to-day affairs of the enterprise and force them to execute their views and ideas.

The respondents expressed that women entrepreneurs do not enjoy economic freedom to the fullest extent. It is also interesting to note that women entrepreneurs are at the mercy of husbands and men folk and they have to get the approval of their men folk in order to dispose even their personal property or jewellery to invest in their venture. Further, it is also ascertained that the family members do not encourage women when they venture out to start an enterprise. At times, the entire family stands as one unit against the woman member. Even when she becomes a successful entrepreneur, the family fails to encourage her to go further and further to achieve greater targets.

There is a general feeling that women may not have risk bearing capacity, self-confidence and they may have the fear of social security to travel and involve in business dealings during nights and odd hours. But it is exciting to note that the respondents are aware of the risk involved in the business and they are courageous enough to face any situation with confidence.

Suggestions

The following suggestions are given in order to overcome the constraints of women entrepreneurs and to elevate the socio-economic status of women, which in turn will lead to the economic growth and overall development of the nation:

1. In Tiruchendur, the potentialities of women entrepreneurs are not properly identified. Hence the government and other agencies should conduct programmes to identify the potentialities of women who could become entrepreneurs;
2. Though the respondents are aware of the banking procedures to get loan, they feel that the procedures are complicated and time consuming. Hence, the procedures and formalities of the bank should be simplified and the required documents should be minimised. Moreover, all the documents shall be in regional language;
3. Women generally do not have their own money. In such cases, women with similar interests and economic background can form groups so as to share knowledge and investment instead of establishing independent enterprises. They may deal with group activity namely group entrepreneurship. There are women organisations like Lioness Club, Self Help Group, and the like. They can provide necessary guidance and other information to the women entrepreneurs;
4. When women work outside their home, they face the problem of dual role and they are in a conflicting frame of mind whether to give priority to home or career. Hence, husbands and men folk should share the household activities;
5. In Tiruchendur, there are educational institutions offering management courses. The government in collaboration with these colleges can overcome the constraint of lack of exposure, by proper refreshing of knowledge through entrepreneurship development

programmes. In this regard training programmes may be arranged;

6. In Tiruchendur, there is no association of women entrepreneurs. They can form an association and meet at a central place on a regular basis so as to discuss their needs, problems, experiences and achievements;

7. Husbands and men folk should be made to realise the significance of women entrepreneurship. Then, their attitude, role and expectation will change and they will provide the necessary capital, guidance and moral support needed by the women folk.

Conclusion

The growth of women entrepreneurs is slow in India and in the case of rural women entrepreneurs; it is very slow and even negligible due to various constraints. The existence of these constraints affects the emergence of women entrepreneurs. In a developing country like India, if effective and concrete steps are taken to overcome the constraints encountered by women entrepreneurs, more women can be brought into the entrepreneur arena. Further, huge employment opportunities can also be generated among the rural women and the poverty can be eradicated among the rural masses.

Reference

1. Maheswari, B.L., "Innovations in Management for Development", Tata McGraw-Hill Publishing Co. Ltd., New Delhi, May 1992.
2. Vasant Desai, "Dynamics of Entrepreneurial Development and Management", Himalaya Publishing House, Delhi, 1992.
3. Gulab Singh Azad, "Development of Entrepreneurship Among Rural Women—An Overview", SEDME, Vol. 15, No. 2, June 1988.
4. Chidambaram, K. and Thenmozhi, G., "Constraints for Women Entrepreneurs", Social Welfare, Vol. 45, No. 1, April 1998.
5. Joshi, J.V. and Madhuri Deshpande, "Study of Women Entrepreneurship in Marathwada", Indian Journal of Marketing, Vol. 32, No. 5-6, May-June 2002.
6. Jubilee Navaprabha, "Development of Rural Women Entrepreneurs in India", Indian Commerce Bulletin, Vol. 6, No. 2, December 2002.

APPENDIX

Garrets Ranking Table

Percentage	Score	Percentage	Score
0.09	99	52.02	49
0.20	98	54.03	48
0.32	97	56.03	47
0.45	96	58.03	46
0.61	95	59.99	45
0.78	94	61.94	44
0.97	93	63.85	43
1.18	92	65.75	42
1.42	91	67.48	41
1.68	90	69.39	40
1.96	89	71.14	39
2.28	88	72.85	38
2.63	87	74.52	37
3.01	86	76.12	36
3.43	85	77.68	35
3.89	84	79.12	34
4.38	83	80.61	33
4.92	82	81.99	32
5.51	81	83.31	31
6.14	80	84.56	30
6.81	79	85.75	29
7.55	78	86.89	28
8.33	77	87.96	27
9.17	76	88.97	26
10.16	75	89.94	25
11.03	74	90.83	24
12.04	73	91.67	23

13.11	72	92.45	22
14.25	71	93.19	21
15.44	70	93.86	20
16.69	69	94.49	19
18.01	68	95.08	18
19.39	67	95.62	17
20.93	66	96.11	16
22.32	65	96.57	15
23.88	64	96.99	14
25.48	63	97.37	13
27.15	62	97.72	12
28.86	61	98.04	11
30.61	60	98.32	10
32.42	59	98.58	9
34.25	58	98.82	8
36.15	57	99.03	7
38.06	56	99.22	6
40.01	55	99.39	5
41.97	54	99.55	4
43.97	53	99.68	3
45.97	52	99.80	2
47.98	51	99.91	1
50.00	50	100	0

Source: Henry, E. Garrett's, Statistics in Psychology and Education, Feffer and Simans Private Limited, 1969, p. 329.

A Study on Women Entrepreneurship

R. Prakash Babu

Studies on women entrepreneurship of industrially less developed areas are very limited because of lack of women entrepreneurs in such areas. However there are sample studies in metropolitan and other capital cities where in women are engaged in some kind of entrepreneurial activities.

Objectives

1. To study qualities of women entrepreneurs and search for potentialities amongst women for entrepreneurship development;
2. To study problems of women entrepreneurs in promoting their units at various stages;
3. To suggest guidelines for growth of women entrepreneurship in a backward region.

Coverage of the Study

1. Majority of the women entrepreneurs were housewives, prior to starting their enterprises. Therefore it is concluded that housewives may be potential source of entrepreneurship;
2. Entrepreneurial mind-set in women due to socio-economic compulsions, has gone into a state of hibernation is induced and activated it can bring

about balances and stable growth women have learnt to be patient due to sustained subordination to men;

Their openness to new ideas is another trait development in them due to their secondary position all through. They have learnt the skill of management from house hold. What is needed is the confidence which the community should supplement in order to enable them to take up. Entrepreneurial ventures since the problem of "Lack of courage and fear of failure" was ranked second.

3. Development is a bilateral phenomenon of giving opportunity and taking opportunity. In case of development of women entrepreneurship the first condition of giving opportunity is at a stage of near fulfillment and the other condition of taking opportunity by the women to be entrepreneur is at a stage of take off. Society at large has not only accepted the rate of women as entrepreneur but it has created an atmosphere conducive for development and emergence of women entrepreneurship;

4. For a woman to assume the role of an entrepreneur become difficult on account of:

   (a) Womenhood and household responsibilities. Women entrepreneurs agree with the statement "First priority of a woman is her home";

   (b) The long cherished role of mother, housewife hampers her from devoting full time efforts for her entrepreneurial role;

   (c) Cultural inhibition imposed on a woman at large is another barricade for her to assume entrepreneurial role.

Other problems of women entrepreneurs are problem of finance, scarcity of raw materials, stiff competition, lack of education and male dominated society.

Development of Women Entrepreneurs

The Government of India has been assigning increasing importance to the development of women entrepreneurs in the country in recent years. The Sixth Five-year Plan for example proposed for promoting female employment in women owned industries. The Government moved a step forward in the Seventh Five-year Plan by including a special chapter of integration of women in development. The chapter suggested:

(a) To treat women as specific target groups in all development programmes.

(b) To provide assistance for marketing their products;

(c) To involve women in decision-making process.

In the industrial policy 1991, the Government of India further stressed the need for conducting special entrepreneurship development programmes for women with a view to encourage women to enter industry.

Guidelines

1. Training programmes should develop self-confidence, self-esteem, assertiveness, courage and risk for women entrepreneurs;
2. Because of womenhood, women have some strength and some weaknesses. Training programme should be designed in such a manner that women entrepreneurs can benefit out of their strength, and overcome their weaknesses;
3. Lack of information and skills for choosing an activity is another major hurdle for development of women entrepreneurship. So training programmes should provide special assistance for selection of produce/service. So that women entrepreneurs can be in a position to perceive and respond to various profitable opportunities;
4. There is an urgent need to educate women for taking up entrepreneurship and for stressing benefits of entrepreneurship. This awareness can be achieved through conferences, seminars, training programmes, refresher courses, awareness camps and other related activities;

5. When women work outside their home, they face problems of childcare. Governmental and other non-Governmental organization should make efforts to provide facilities in the form of child care institutions like crèches, nurseries and child care facilities. These facilities should adjust timings, locations as per the convenience of women entrepreneurs;

6. Success stories of women entrepreneurs from varied backgrounds should be popularized through textbooks of schools and colleges. All possible media should be used to project these role models;

7. For economic security of women, it is necessary to develop co-operative credit societies where small amounts of money can be saved and used for giving better financial resources to women. This process would develop intended support among its members;

8. Illiterate women generally work in household enterprises. They find it difficult to interact with the outside environment because of lack of courage and fear of failure. So such women should be trained in modern techniques and latest trends in activities like sewing, dairy, bakery, spinning, weaving, leather products etc. so that productive utilization of their time and capacities can take place.

For stimulating entrepreneurship among women significant efforts have been made by a number of departments of Central and State Governments in terms of offering incentives/benefits. Even the industrial policies, five-year plans emphasize the promotion of women entrepreneurship. A variety of programmes have been under-taken by a multitude of organizations with the intention of stimulating women entrepreneurship. But to ensure that these benefits will reach the common women to ensure an attitudinal change in regard to the role of women as an entrepreneur will certainly lead to the development of a conducive environment in which women entrepreneurship will flourish like anything. Business entrepreneurship provides economic independence and social status to women. Ultimately it leads to future economic prosperity of the nation.

Socio-economic Constraints of Women Entrepreneur

Sr. Josephine Nirmala,
V. Sathuragiri

Introduction

India is mainly an agricultural country and a very large number of people are engaged in agricultural occupation. The Rural sector in India also plays a predominant role in the development of the economy. In the rural area, rural women constitute nearly 50 per cent of the country's population. They have been neglected from enjoying even their fundamental rights till recent times. Since independence the government has been introducing several schemes for their all-round development, but the results are not upto the mark.

Rural Women

Rural women play a major role in developing the economy and to participate in all stages. They have been the invisible contributors to the production process. There has been a lack of proper organisation. Women were endowed with entrepreneurial skills, particularly in business. Basically women's status in the society was not satisfactory. The credit facilities were not extended to women. They were uneducated and they depended upon their husbands and parents. These are the reasons why women did not enter into business. These have been eliminated through forming voluntary association i.e. SHGs.

Self Help Groups

SHG is a suitable means for the empowerment of women. The SHGs started playing an important role in the rural development. It is a voluntary group in a particular village. Those who are below the poverty level joined together under one banner. They pay some subscription towards savings and with this accumulated amount, credit is given to group members at a very low rate of interest for starting new business.

Status in Tamil Nadu

As far as Tamil Nadu is concerned, the Government of Tamil Nadu established a separate wing called "Tamil Nadu Corporation for Women Development Ltd" in 1983, to form SHGs through the scheme called Mahalir Thittam (MATHI). Though the scheme was launched in 1996-97, it began its operation from 1997-98 onwards.

The main objectives of the corporation are:

- Focus on empowerment of women;
- To build capacity of women to enable them to participate in the mainstream activities;
- To promote entrepreneurship among women;
- To identify trades and industries which can be taken by women and giving them training in the chosen fields;
- To undertake marketing activities for products manufactured by women and their organisations;
- To form SHGs for poor women both in rural and urban areas, develop skills, and facilitate credit linkage for eventual economic empowerment.

Six schemes are being implemented by DeW (Development of Women) in pursuance of the above objectives.

In a traditionally conservative society in Tamil Nadu, risk-aversion is common. Women are a further help behind the average man, having to contend with gender barriers in financial institutions, discouragement in families, lower levels of education and confidence. DeW proposes to break such barriers by a facilitative approach through SHGs.

- Build capacity of NGOs for supporting entrepreneurship among women;
- Training in business management for women;
- Skill upgradation for women;

DeW has commenced the following:

- 4 stages of training of Trainers' courses have been conducted by NGO trainers for promoting micro-enterprises among women;
- A training manual for the use of NGO trainers while training SHGs taking up micro-enterprises is under development.

Sample Survey

An attempt has been made to study the role of SHGs functioning in Theni District (TN) in income generation and problem of the poor rural women through SHG. Tamil Nadu has 26220 SHGs as on 31.03.2000. Among the total, the selected district, Theni has 2097 SHGs as on 31.10.02. There are 8 blocks in the districts viz., Aundipatti, K. Myladumparai, Periyakulam, Bodi, Chinnamunur, Uttamapalayam, Cumbum and Theni. Of these blocks, Bodi has been chosen for the present study. The present study is conducted in relation to AHM Trust voluntary organisation. Bodi has 135 SHGs with 2173 women members. 50 were selected from AHMT taking into consideration the tenure of membership as the strata. For the economic development of the SHG members, during 2000-2001. Rs. 2,05,000 were spent for increasing the income generation activities. All SHG members have been benefited by these activities.

Table 3.1 shows the various activities of the AHM Trust and the amount spent on such activities.

Table 3.1. Activities of AHM and Amount Spent during 2001-2002

Sl. No	Activities	Amount Rs.	Percentage
1.	Cows rearing	69,000	33.65
2.	Goat rearing	49,000	23.90
3.	Tailoring	18,000	8.78
4.	Idli shop	11,000	5.37
5.	Petty shop	8,000	3.90
6.	Cloth Business	7,000	3.41
7.	Calf Rearing	6,000	2.92
8.	Dairy Business	5,000	2.44
9.	Vegetable Business	5,000	2.44
10.	Grinding Machine	2,000	0.98
11.	Ration shop	25,000	12.20
		2,05,000	100

Source: Secondary Data.

It is evident from Table 3.1 that a majority of the amount of 33.65 per cent has been spent on cows rearing and 23.90 per cent on goat rearing. A least amount of 0.98 per cent has been spent on grinding machine.

Many SHG women members are currently involved with some additional economic activities such as making agarbathis, production of candle and soap, readymade garments, pickles, apalam, vathal, toys, bags, palm leaf products, sarees, dhotis, herbal products, fancy sea shell ornaments, eatables, coir matt and other coir products, mattresses, chappals and leader goods, milk business. Majority of the SHG members are earning not less than Rs. 1,000 p.m. as their income.

The constraints encountered by the Women Entrepreneur, are many. As far as this study is concerned, only the personal and social constraints are tabulated amount. After a pretest with the help of an interview to be a list containing all entrepreneurial constraints have been prepared.

The seriousness of constraints have been studied on the basis of the overall mean score which were ranked on the basis of mean score.

$$\text{Mean} = \frac{\text{Total scores}}{\text{No. of respondents}}$$

The respondents were divided into two categories of yes and no and weights as one and zero respectively were assigned.

Personal Constraints

Table 3.2 exhibits the various personal constraints of Women Entrepreneur.

Table 3.2. Personal Constraints of Women Entrepreneurs

Sl. No	Constraints	Mean score	Rank
1.	Problems connected with health	0.75	II
2.	Lack of leisure time	0.53	XII
3.	Excessive Tensions & challenges	0.54	X.1
4.	Capacity to work hard	0.76	I
5.	Incapacity to take risk	0.42	XV
6.	Unsystematic planning & working	0.60	VIII
7.	Self motivation	0.69	IV
8.	Excessive burden of work and excessive reasonability	0.66	V
9.	Difficulty in handling technical and managerial activities	0.49	XIV
10.	Improper training	0.62	VI
11.	Lack of organisation skill	0.51	XIII
12.	Absence of financial assistance	0.54	X.1
13.	Raw material availability	0.61	VII
14.	No knowledge on competition	0.55	IX
15.	No knowledge on legal assets	0.72	III
	Overall Mean score	0.60	

It is clear from the above Table 3.2, among the various personal constraints of women entrepreneurs, capacity to workhard and problems connected with health, were the most common constraints.

Socio-economic Constraints

Table 3.3 exhibits the various Socio and Economic constraints of women entrepreneur.

Table 3.3. Socio-economic Constraints of Women Entrepreneur

So. No	Socio-economic constraints	Mean score	Rank
1.	Lack of appreciation	0.78	II
2.	Labour problem	0.48	XIV
3.	Inadequate infrastructure	0.58	VIII
4.	Marketing problem	0.50	XII
5.	Transport problem	0.52	X
6.	Lack of self confidence	0.60	VII
7.	Lack of encouragement	0.49	XIII
8.	Problem of mobility	0.53	IX
9.	Social status	0.74	III
10.	Lack of sufficient time	0.65	V
11.	Problem of purlic relation	0.51	I
12.	In discipline	0.42	XV
13.	Conflicts due to duel responsibilities	0.80	I
14.	Family size	0.71	IV
15.	Locatisation of business	0.64	VI

It is clear from the Table 3.3 among the various socio-economic of women entrepreneurs conflicts due to duel responsibility was the most common constraints.

Conclusion

Though SHGs are revolutionising the rural economy, it is observed from the field study that SHGs members are suffering from some of the social and economic problems. Now it is the duty of the Government and NGOs to take necessary steps to remove the sufferings of the SHG's members. Once the bottlenecks faced by the SHGs are removed, the growth rate of SHGs will be tremendous. More over the formation of SHGs should also be extended to semi-urban and urban centers. The women in these areas also remain unorganised. They could not avail any of the credit facilities as they engage in entrepreneurial activities individually. Thus the formation SHGs both in rural and Urban centers make the women empowered socially and economically.

Problems and Prospects of Rural Women Entrepreneurs

Dr. S. Maria John,
Mrs. A. Mary Grace

Entrepreneurship

The word 'entrepreneurship' has been derived from a French root which means "to undertake". It is defined by the Encyclopaedia Britannica as an individual responsible for the operation of a business, including the choice of a product, the mobilisation of necessary capital, decisions on product prices and quotations, the employment of labour and expanding or reducing the productive facilities. Today people call it as adventurism, risk taking, thrill seeking, innovating etc.

Rural entrepreneurs are those entrepreneurs who actually hail from and reside in rural areas i.e. either from a panchayat or a Town Panchayat and mobilise human resource requirements from those areas in which they live. Rural business is also rural based and located in rural areas. Rural entrepreneurs are suited for dairying, poultry, processing food products like pickle, papads, tamarind, vegetable, weaving and making of incense sticks.

Concepts of Rural Women Entrepreneurship

A woman entrepreneur is one who owns and controls an enterprise having a share capital of not less than 51 per cent as partners/shareholders/directors of private limited company/ members of Cooperative Societies. Women in India are not now confined to four walls of a house. They are participating well in all spheres of activities such as academic, politics, administration and industry.

Rural Industrialisation and Development

The Indian Government, on seeing the importance and role of rural industries, is allocating higher amount of outlays, which is always on increase, during the plan periods. Table 4.1 provides the plan outlays during the plan periods.

Table 4.1. Plan Outlays for Rural Industrialisation

Sl. No.	Plan Period	Plan Outlays Rs. in Crores	Consultative percentage
1.	First Plan 1951-56	42	0.340
2.	Second Plan 1956-61	187	1.855
3.	Third Plan 1961-66	241	3.806
4.	Annual Plans 1966-69	126	4.827
5.	Fourth Plan 1969-74	293	7.200
6.	Fifth Plan 1974-80	592	11.994
7.	Sixth Plan 1980-85	1,780	26.409
8.	Seventh Plan 1985-90	2,753	48.704
9.	Eighth Plan 1990-93	6,334	100.000
	Growth rate in Percentage	15,081	

Source: Five Year Plans, Planning Commission 1989-90, Vol. 1
Growth rate is calculated as yt/yo x 100.

Table 4.1 shows that there has been huge allotment of money towards rural industrialisation over a period of 43 years. It is also evident from the cumulative percentage and the growth rate.

As far as the rural development of India in general and Tamil Nadu in particular, is concerned the Government of India has been allotting large sums towards its growth and development through the annual and five year plans. The allotment of funds for rural development over a period of three years is given in Table 4.2.

Table 4.2. Availability and Utilisation of Funds for Rural Development to Tamil Nadu

Rs. in crores

Sl. No.	Period	Plan outlay	Plan expenditure	Total funds available	Funds Utilised
1.	1997-1998	4005	4011	1019	1156
2.	1998-1999	4500	4516	1058	1121
3.	1999-2000	5250	5250	829	992

Source: Five Year Plans, Planning Commission, New Delhi 1999-2000.

Though Globalisation has become a red-herring in the development debate in the country, it has outlayed a lot over the annual plans just to place the country in an elevated plane through various schemes for rural development. Consequently the Small and Rural Industries have grown in number, shown large production, employment and have resulted in increased exports.

Though the Rural male entrepreneurs are dominating the field of business, women rural entrepreneurs are no less endowed with qualities that contribute to successful entrepreneurship. Prospective Rural Women Entrepreneurs who promote entrepreneurship amongst their men folk are also to be influenced to secure support to the venture.

Women entrepreneurs are motivated by internal factors such as the family background, education background and the desire to do something independently. Except those women from upper and middle classes i.e. the women from economically lower classes have worked on farms and also taken to other occupation involving physical work. Consequent to the increase in women's education, social and educational mobility, industrialisation and urbanisation, women have taken up a number of vocations.

Area Profile

The study area, Kanyakumari District has a total population of 16,00,349. Of the total population a majority reside in rural areas. The district has 4 taluks viz. Agasteeswaram Taluk, Vilavancode Taluk, Kalkulam Taluk and Thovalai Taluk. Kalkulam Taluk covers more rural areas in the district and stands first in rural population also. This Taluk has more rural population than others. In this Taluk around 350 entrepreneurs are engaged in Dairy farming. 78 entrepreneurs are women who actually engage themselves in rearing cows. Of the 78 women entrepreneurs 15 (20%) have been selected. Of this 15, entrepreneurs 10 entrepreneurs are doing the business without any principal investment of their own.

In the area selected for the study there are other women entrepreneurs who are engaged in other businesses like food products production, and processing like crystal sugar, tamarind, provision, tapioca chips, tailoring, soap manufacturing, beedi manufacturing and the like.

The objective of the study is to analyse the various problems faced by the women rural entrepreneurs engaged in dairy farming and its allied activities and to suggest possible remedial measures to overcome.

Mode of Operation and the Allied Activities

In this study, rural women entrepreneurs who are engaged in dairy farming, with a maximum of three or more cows for their existence is taken into account. Their life partners and paid labourers are helping them in marketing the dairy products. These people are dealing with the following activities.

Decide finally to do such a venture;

Arrange for finance to construct the cow shed;

Arrange for finance to buy the cows;

Procurement of cows, cattle feed and straw;

Rearing of cows and get the yield (milk).

They also make use of the milk in preparing butter, butter milk, ghee, cheese, etc., and preparing manure with animal wastes. Thus from the above ways and means (allied activities) they generate income to the business. This income is allocated in the following ways:

Table 4.3. Table Showing Allocation of Income

Sl. No.	Pattern	Percentage
1.	Repayment of bank loan, received to procure cows and construct the shed	15%
2.	Repayment of instalment due on purchase of cattle feeds	5%
3.	Maintaining of cows (medical)	5%
4.	Maintaining the family	46.5%
5.	Interest on private borrowing	28.5%
	Total	**100**

Source: Primary Data.

Role of Milk Collection Methods

In the selected areas milk has been sold twice a day, by the following methods:

1. *Spot procurement*

The private milk societies or registered dairy cooperative societies visit the houses of the entrepreneurs and collect milk twice a day.

2. *Local distribution (Centralised)*

The entrepreneurs sell milk to the local milk consumers by keeping the milk at their farms. Various milk consumers come to the farm and buy milk, both in the morning and evening.

3. *Local distribution (De-centralised)*

According to the needs of the milk consumers, the entrepreneurs visit the houses of the milk consumers and supply milk daily.

4. *Private milk vendors*

The entrepreneurs also sell milk to the private milk vendors in bulk, carrying the milk to the place of the private milk vendors, who sometimes sell in the neighbouring states.

5. ***At the door of the societies (Late Sales)***

Some entrepreneurs sell milk only in the local villages. During some occasions i.e., if the production is more or when there is less sales there will be unsold milk (surplus). This surplus is sold to the societies at the door. Only a very few sell the milk to producers who use milk as raw materials for milk products (curd, ghee, milk beada, powder etc.,). All the methods have both pros and cons.

A survey of 78 respondents regarding the above mentioned milk collection methods reveals the following figures:

Table 4.4

Sl. No.	Type of Sales	No. of Entrepreneurs	Percentage to Total
1.	Spot procurement (Societies)	29	37.18
2.	Local Distribution Centralised	15	19.23
3.	Local Distribution De-centralised	9	11.54
4.	Private Milk vendor	16	20.51
5.	At the door of Societies	3	3.85
6.	Producers	6	7.69
	Total	**78**	**100.00**

Source: Primary Data.

Cost-Benefit Analysis

The cost per liter of milk comes around to Rs. 7.50 to the entrepreneur taking into account the overall cost incurred on the cattles from its procurement to the yield. On an average one entrepreneur gets only Rs. 1.50 per litre. The milk procurement rate is Rs. 9 per litre. An entrepreneur gets an average of 10 litres of milk per day, thereby a total yield of Rs. 15 from a single cow and Rs. 45 from 3 cows. He has to apportion this amount on the above said five ways. It is felt by all the entrepreneurs that the reward they get is inadequate to the efforts they take in this respect.

Table 4.5. Cost Analysis of Milk

Sl. No.	Particulars	Cost Price Rs.	Selling Price Rs.	Margin Rs.
1.	Cost per litre of milk	7.50	9.00	1.50
2.	Cost per cow @ an average of 10 litres per day	75.00	90.00	15.00
3.	Cost per day @ 3 cows @ 10 litres per cow	225.00	270.00	45.00
4.	Cost per day @ 3 cows @ 270 days	20,250.00	24,300.00	4,050.00
5.	Cost per issue per cow @ 270 days @ 3 cows	60,750.00	72,900.00	12,150.00

Source: Primary Data.

Cost Price = Cost of maintenance + Cost of fodder + Interest on investments

Selling price = Milk Procurement Price

Margin = Net return to the entrepreneur

There are two types of entrepreneurs in this field. The aforesaid cost analysis pertains to the first category of entrepreneurs who do not have principal investment of their own in the business. As they borrow even for the construction of shed, maintenance etc., the margin per litre is Rs. 1.50 only. The second category of entrepreneurs are those who do the business hereditarily and have a primary fodder requirement from own fields. As they need not spend more on fodder, their maintenance cost is lower to a certain extent. They get an average of Rs. 2.50 to Rs. 3.00 as surplus margin per litre.

Problems

Role of Private Milk Vendors

The private milk vendors working in villages and towns play a dominant role in exploiting the rural entrepreneurs. The reason being, these people liberally grant advance for purchase of animals. These people fix the price for milk on the basis of the fat content on the milk. As the poor illiterate entrepreneurs are unaware of the method of measurement of fat content, they are very often exploited by fixing low price to their milk.

Quality of Animals

Productivity depends on quality of animals. High breed animals give more output per day. However people of the study area do not prefer the high breed animals as the cost of such animals is high. Further the prevailing climatic conditions and the cow rearing habits followed by these people may not be suitable for profitable farming. That is why the people of this area prefer low breed and mixed breed animals which results in low productivity.

Rearing of Young Ones

The entrepreneurs are always in financially strain. They have to meet with various kinds of personal commitments with the help of the margin on milk. So they try to make maximum use of the cattle by taking the entire milk from the cows without leaving at least a little to the calves. During the infant stage, the calves are more dependent on their mother feed. When their staple, food i.e. milk is denied they become weak.

Unwise Applications of Business Receipts

Entrepreneurs engaged in dairy farming often fail to keep the business as a separate entity. Due to perennial financial strain, they used to club their personal commitments with the income from dairy business. This results in unwise utilisation of business receipts to meet the domestic requirements. This practice ultimately leads the people falling in permanent debt-trap.

Unhygienic Surroundings

The shed surroundings is also unhygienic because of the overcrowded situation prevailing in the areas where they reside. The sheds have to be kept clean daily and they are required to be sprayed with anti insecticides. This unhealthy surroundings affect the milk production to a certain extent.

Death of Cattle

Demise of cattle due to unhygienic surroundings and non efficient rearing are a common phenomenon in villages. They do not have the knowledge to insure their cattle to restrain away from such a loss. Loss of a cow means loss of fixed Asset. Calves also die due to lack of balanced basic diet. As most of the entrepreneurs are low educated they very often call the sub-staff of the Animal Husbandry Department for treatment to their cattles.

Financial Commitment

Indian farmers born in debt, live in debt and die in debt. Likewise entrepreneurs too face always financial problems. During contingencies they are found at the door of the money lenders. The entrepreneurs sell the milk on credit. They procure the cattle feed on credit. They sometimes give advance to the workers, out of the borrowed money, which is a double burden.

The financial assistance to the entrepreneurs from many regulated financial institutions under various schemes is found to be insufficient for them, they solely depend on the income from this business even for family maintenance. Consequently they go in search of money lenders. Very often these money lenders happen to be those in the same line of business. In these circumstances the entrepreneurs are forced to get the fodder from them and give the entire yield to these lenders, thereby creating a clutch.

Settlement

The settlement of accounts, for the milk sold to the Co-operative Societies, usually takes place once in a month. As these people are accustomed to daily/weekly borrowings. This type of monthly settlement of accounts results in high cost of production. But in private procurement, the entrepreneurs are allowed to avail settlement according to their choice. So entrepreneurs are easily attracted towards such private parties.

It has been found out in the study area that the women entrepreneurs work hard and enjoy the benefit and help their families. Most of their family members are depending on them. But these people are not concerned cared, regarded and recognised by the depending the family members. This treatment wounds the entrepreneurs psychologically to a certain extent.

Suggestions

In order to give a fillip to the entrepreneurs who are engaged in dairy farming, in the study area, the following remedial steps are suggested. The Dairy Co-operative Societies can supply high quality cattle feed at subsidised rate from the government or agencies established to support the Dairy farming. Always there should be timely disbursement of loans and the supply of cattle feed. The individual entrepreneurs (residing in far away places) do not have storage facilities. In this connection, Co-operative Societies can play a positive role, in the line private milk societies perform.

A recent survey conducted in among the Asian and Australian countries has proved that, 56 and of the Indian males believe their wives to share with secrets and other life commitments. In this situation the sample entrepreneurs family members can change themselves to believe, support and recognize the earning entrepreneurs.

The Central and State Governments have been imparting training and Research Oriented programmes throughout the country. The younger generation i.e., the employed youth can make use of these programmes not only in cattle rearing, but also in production of milk and meat products, hybrid, pisiculture, growing colour fish, poultry farming etc. Lessons relating to cattle rearing are also taught through the All India Radio during April to June every year.

Insurance is a social device where a large group of persons, through a system of equitable distribution, reduce or eliminate certain measurable risks of economic loss common to all members of the group. Loss of cattle is a measurable risk but an immeasurable loss to the entrepreneur. So insurance of cattle will wither away the loss of cattle caused to the entrepreneurs. The insurance authorities can educate the poor entrepreneurs regarding importance of insurance by pamphlets, public announcement, multimedia, dramas, workshops etc.,

The social welfare organisations functioning in villages can organise for free medical camps for the cattles twice in a week in consultation with the Department of Animal

Husbandry. These organisations can also arrange for giving free goats and hybrid variety hens to the existing entrepreneurs who can increase their income in one way or other, thereby paving way for mixed farming. This income from such other source will definitely reduce the family burden and default in repayment of loans borrowed.

Lack of saving habit is the root cause of over spending, when the above measures are implemented the poor entrepreneurs can reduce the expenditure on the various heads and will see surplus in their hands. This situation will induce the saving habit among them. During this phase they can be advised to provide for more savings and more allotment towards contingencies. More allotment towards contingencies will reduce most of the risks faced by the entrepreneurs. Through the habit of savings the entrepreneurs can seen that they easily overcome even the family maintenance problems and get a status in the society.

The government while granting loans under various financial schemes with subsidy should attach a provision for savings at the time of repayment. This savings, in the long run would prove to be self-supporting the entrepreneurs. The social organisations, village sangoms and voluntary agencies functioning in the villages should educate the illiterate entrepreneurs regarding the benefits of (1) keeping the cows, calves and surroundings clean and tidy, (2) effect of saving in the long run, (3) feeding the cows in time and the quantity of food and (4) they can see that the poor entrepreneurs are free to avail the various financial loan schemes and subsidy without the unnecessary costly involvement and interference of the government officials.

The womenfolk at rural areas who are interested in cow rearing and actually in this cow rearing profession should form Self Help Groups among themselves. It will help them to avail easy credit facilities from the Banks. Thus they can escape from the clutches of private milk vendor. Such a joint effort will help them to go for producers of value added products of milk like butter, ghee, milk beda etc., which will fetch more income to the women entrepreneurs of such Self Help Groups.

Reference

1. *The Dina Thanthi, "Youth Malar"* dated 28th April 2001, Nagarcoil.
2. Entrepreneurship Development, Colombo Plan Staff College for Technician Education—Manila, Centre for Research and Industrial Staff Performance—Bhopal.
3. Mervin C.L. Financing of Small Corporations pp. 15-24.
4. Mamoria, CB and Tripathi, BB Agricultural Problems of India, Kithab Mahal, Allahabad 1997.
5. *The Hindu* dated December 16, 2000, Madurai.

Women Entrepreneurs in Rural India

Mrs. V. Kavitha,
R. Anitha

Introduction

Men have not been fair to the fair sex in economic life. Average women's earnings in most countries is lower than those of men. In many developing countries, marriage is the only carrier for most women. Professionally women have confined their activities to such areas as education, office work, nursing and medicine. It is only rarely that they enter professions like engineering, business, etc. Though women constitute almost half of the world population, their representation in gainful employment is comparatively low. An I.L.O report in 1980 states that "Women are 50 per cent of the world's population, do the two-thirds of the world's work hours, receives 10 per cent of world's income and not less than 1 per cent of world property. All because of an accident of birth". As regards, India, women constitute 60 per cent of the rural unemployment and 56 per cent of the total unemployed.

In traditional societies women had been confined to the four-walls of home, children, household affairs and family rituals and customs. Very few had the opportunity to come out of the four walls and shine in different spheres.

In recent years women have come in forefront in different walks of life and all competing successfully with men despite the social, psychological and economic barriers.

Growth Awareness in India

Having realised the importance of the role to be played by women in the nation's development, in the Seventh Five Year Plan, a special chapter on women's development has been included and it details the plan of action for "Integration of Women in development". The New Industrial Policy of Government of India specially highlighted the need for conducting special entrepreneurship programmes for women which would be in the nature of product/process oriented courses meant for women entrepreneurs to enable them to start small scale industries with a view to uplifting their status in economic and social fields.

It is only during the last 5-10 years women have started becoming entrepreneurs and started and businesses and they are yet to go a long way to be at par with men. The situation is quite understandable, as women have to play a dual role as a housewife and also as an income earner. Thus arise a role conflict—many a women, which prevent them from taking a prompt decision in entering the business. Despite the modernization and other factors mentions, the weight of tradition and the responsibilities the women have to discharge to their children as mother slows down this movement. Further, occupational backgrounds of the families and the educational attainment of the husbands have a direct bearing in the development of women entrepreneurship.

Training Organizations

There are agencies such as Small Industries Service Institute (SISIs) and branch SISIs and Technical Consultancy Organisations, Industrial Consultant at region wise and National Small Industries Corporation (NSIC). In addition, in 1993, Government of India setup Indian Institute of Entrepreneurship (IIE), a national institute to act as catalyst on entrepreneurship development.

The implementation of Prime Minister's Rozgar Yojana (PMRY) from 1993 led the District Industries Centres (DIC's), Small Industries Development Corporations (SIDCs), National

Productivity Council (NPC), Small Industries associations and non-governmental organisations, consultants, etc., to take of PMRY beneficiaries. There are how voluntary organisations also who are directly involved in promotion of entrepreneurship through training and support.

Emerging Trends

The efforts to promote and develop entrepreneurship during the last more than two and half decades have resulted in some changes in the entrepreneurial scenario.

Information Technology has become a potent force in transforming social, economic and political life globally and without its incorporation it is difficult for countries or regions to develop if not to survive. Inspite of some sceptical arguments against the relevance of information technology in Indian conditions, many people are hopeful of exploiting its potential to spur not only growth in national economy as a whole, but also to bring in new opportunities to those who are mired in despair.

IT for Empowerment of Women

The most outstanding feature of the firm empowerment is that it contains within it, the word power. Empowerment, is about power and about changing the balance of power.

The empowerment process is one where women find time and space of their own, and bring to reexamine their lives critically and collectively. They enable women to look at old problems in new ways, analyse their environment and situation, recognise their strength, alter their self-image, access new kinds of information and knowledge, acquire new skills and initiate action aimed at gaining greater control over resources of various kinds.

As the women empowerment is concerned it is about gaining autonomy and control over one's life which includes many dimensions. Women's empowerment is a state of being that reflects a certain level of critical consciousness about internal realities and an awareness about their internal thought construction and belief systems that affect their well being in terms of gender justice and social justice, as well as the determination to use their physical, intellectual, emotional and spiritual resources to protect their lives and sustain values that guarantee gender equity at personal, social, economic, political and institutional level.

The need to use information technology in empowering women can be understood in two fold manner. So far no other technology claimed to have given the instant, uncensored, practically feasible, economically viable information to the women folk that the information technology.

The IT poses new forms of learning education, health services, livelihood options and e-commerce options which would lead to the ultimate goal (i.e.,) women's empowerment.

The second reason why IT should be used for women's empowerment is something to do with the digital divide. The uneven distribution of IT within societies lead to digital divide between the informations "haves" and "have not". The access to and use of information technology is directly linked to social and economic development, then it is imperative to ensure that women in India understand the significance of IT and use them. If not, the other end.

One of the most powerful application of IT is electronic commerce. E-commerce, in the context of women empowerment, refers not just to selling of products and services online but to the promotion of a new class of IT array women the entrepreneurial behaviours of women by improving their innovativeness, decision making ability, access to various services and ability to co-ordinate the activities and people. Besides, it provides information to small business owners especially women which will be helpful in expanding their horizons.

Women entrepreneurs in India can secure gains from IT with little technical training. After an Internet training workshop for members of the Association for Support to Women Entrepreneurs [ASAFE] in Cameroon, Bio-vital, an ASAFE member that manufactures cosmetics made from local herbs and plants, used the Internet to locate a French company that now buys 80 per cent of its production.

In a remote village in Guyana, women formed an organization called Rupumumi Weavers Society to receive the ancient art of hand weaving large hammocks from locally grown cotton. Then they marketed hand weaven hammocks over the Internet of $1000 each; which is enormous compared to local standards.

Another important area is core IT sector empowerment. There are significant opportunities for women in Software. Network Administration, education and training, etc., are the areas of IT where can benefit enormously.

Women can act as Information intermediaries between the Internet and the rural people. These women can be agricultural extension agents, community workers of Internet operators who can get useful information from Internet and pass on the same to the local people. They assist in the two communication and helps in Internet vice-versa people's interaction. By doing so they can earn some amount of money leading to enhance economic contribution of women.

Information revolution, though is recent and juvenile, is ever expanding in its premises and challenges. Information is power and acquisition of relevant information, at opportune time will facilitate decision making and empowerment.

Conclusion

In the present context of rapidly changing world, where societal transformations are called for, there is no other potential tool other than information technology, for empowering the most deprived section, i.e., women. An effective policy towards initiating socially acceptable, economically viable and practically feasible IT projects will be a major step in realising the social, political and economic empowerment of women. The concept of "leap frogging" is not only applicable in bridging the divide between developed and developing world, but also bridging the social divide between the empowered and disempowered.

Opportunities for Women Entrepreneurs in Rural India

M. Padmini

Introduction

Mahatma Gandhiji underlined the importance of rural areas by saying that India lives in villages. The role of village and cottage industries in rural development is considered as vital as these are the very backbone of the Indian rural economic with 74 per cent of our population still living in rural areas. India is predominantly an *Agrarian* society, this agriculture has provided much more employment opportunities in the village for rural youth and women.

Concept of Women Entrepreneurs

Women Entrepreneurs are the women or a group of women who initiate, organize and operate a business enterprise. The Government of India notes women entrepreneurs as

> "an enterprise owned and controlled by women saving a minimum financial interest of 51 per cent of the capital and giving at least 51 per cent of the employment generated in the enterprise to women".

Emerging Women Entrepreneurs

The emergence of women entrepreneur depends on religious environmental socio-economic and psychological factors it is grouped under "pull factors" and "push factors".

Pull factors refers to the urge in women to undertake a venture with an inclination to start a business.

Push factors refers women entering business, driven by financial need due to family circumstances.

Opportunities for Rural Women Entrepreneurs

It is most important to create a favourable atmosphere for a healthy development of women's entrepreneurship we have an example of Kerala, how they work in a favourable atmosphere since last two decades. In 1975-76 the number of industrial units run by women entrepreneurs in Kerala was 73. It has increased to 4190 industrial units in 1993-94. The women entrepreneurs in Kerala are now at the top as all industrial right readymade garments to high-tech computers.

Suitable Rural Entrepreneurial Activities for Women

Selection of suitable industry depends of existing women's entrepreneurial capabilities, family support, and locational advantage and availability of financial and raw material and other infrastructure facilities etc.

Handloom cottage industries, khadi and village industries are providing employment opportunities to women. Entrepreneurship started by women is no longer confined to conventional fields like embroidery, knitting and tailoring or 3P's pickles, powder, and pappad, but women are venturing now it to modern technological field or 3E's Energy, Electricity and Electronics.

But now the scenario is changing fast with modernization, and development of education and business. Thus the opportunities of employment for women have increased drastically. Self employment opportunities are still popular among rural women, they can start poultry, dairy, piggeries, bee-keeping goatry, petty shop keeping match boxes, agarbathy, agriculture and allied operations and establish small units to produce sauce and other similar products in corrective way.

Potential Industrial Opportunities in Theni District

In Theni District we have wide potential industrial opportunities such as:

1. Cattle and poultry feed
2. Leather products (chappls and bags)
3. Agricultural farm implements
4. Bakery products
5. Manufacturing Note Books
6. Pickles and appalams
7. Herbal cultivation and processing
8. Mineral water plant
9. Extraction of coconut oil
10. Coir mat weaving
11. Mango Fruit pulps, juices, jams and squashes
12. Turmeric powder
13. Instant food mix
14. Handlooms
15. Confectioneries

Role of Institution in the Promotion of Rural Women Entrepreneurs

Government recognized rural women as a source of potential entrepreneurs and have initiated many programmes to give financial, managerial, technical and marketing assistance. Various institutions and agencies were set up to give training and financial, marketing assistance to tiny, cottage and village industries.

1. State industrial development corporation
2. District Industrial centre provide assistance through self-employment for educated unemployed youth.

Rural Development Programmes

The main objectives of integrated rural development programmes is to increase the income generating power of the family who are below the poverty line to alleviate the poverty. 30 per cent women should be the beneficiaries in rural development programmes run by the government. The main rural development programmes are:

- Indira Mahila Yojana (IMY)
- Rastria Mahila Kosh (RMK)
- STEP
- NORAD programme

Indira Mahila Yojana (IMY)

Indira mahila yojana was launched in August 1995. Its main objective is to give a forward thrust to education, awareness, income generation capacity and the empowerment to women.

Rastriya Mahila Kosh (RMK)

RMK is also organizing training apprenticeship and orientation programmes, for trainers under Indian Mahila Block Societies (IMBS). The experience of RMK is that the women would have been able to double or triple their dairy income with the credit support of Rs. 2000/or Rs. 5000 the activities followed may be dairying, petty-shop keeping and Investment of the agriculture operations.

STEP

Science and Technology Entrepreneurship Park was started in 1987 with the objective to provide training to rural women for increasing their production capacity and income generation. In this programme, they give training in the areas of traditional business like agriculture, milk, fisheries, handlooms, khadi, development etc.

2.5 lakhs women have been benefited by this programme since its inception. Maximum number of beneficiaries of milk-producing area. In 1996-97 (up to 31st December, 1996) this programme has an expenditure of 1.44 crores and number of beneficiary women are 2490.

NORAD Programme

NORAD stands for Norwegian Agency for International Development, NORAD was established in 1982-83 to help the educated and uneducated women financially in non-traditional areas of business like electronics, computer programming, manufacturing of watches, printing, readymade garments etc. 64200 women are benefited by NORAD programme. In 1996-97 (up to 31st December, 1996) it has an expenditure of 355.91 lakhs and beneficiary women are 6065.

Strategies for Development of Rural Women Entrepreneur

The following strategies may be taken the empowerment of women.

1. Educating girls and women;
2. Facilitating their involvement in economic activities through development of their entrepreneurial and income earning capabilities and access to credit;
3. Involving women in policy formulation and decision making;
4. Encouraging socio-cultural charge by exploiting gender issues and promoting effective implementation of equal rights through legislation;
5. Women expect less formalities in setting up the units, easy and quick processing of assistance from the Government agencies;
6. They must aware of the various Government assistance especially for women.

Conclusion

The participation of women in the economic life of a country necessary for national development. Now the growth of women entrepreneurship has become socio-economic significance in a country like India. By opening a large number of small industrial ventures women entrepreneurs can strengthen the industrial base, provide employment opportunities and achieve balanced growth. Thus, emerging economic force of women entrepreneurs can contribute a lot to industrial development of the country.

Constraints on Rural Women Entrepreneurs—An Experiment Through Micro Credit

Haji Dr. M. Sheik Mohamed
N. Arul Prakash

Introduction

Women groups and NGOs initiated micro credit programmes at local levels as one component of the development strategy to empower poor women. But now-a-days micro credit is no longer a localized activity. For Banks and financial institutions micro credit offers new avenues of profit making since interest rates range from 20 to 40 per cent and repayment rates are over 90 per cent, far above commercial lending.

The most common criterion used for measuring the success of micro credit programmes is the loan repayment rate. The loan repayment rate is very high compared to commercial lending but this does not explain the qualitative impact of such programmes in terms of increasing flows of income, levels of employment and sustainability of businesses. Since the lenders are primarily concerned with repayment of loans, vital issues related to the quality and wider socio-economic impact of such loans have not been given due attention.

Impact of Micro Credit Programmes

The recent studies on impact of micro credit programmes run by Grameen Bank of Bangladesh, one of the pioneers of micro credit, reveal that workers and peer group members put pressure on women borrowers for timely repayment, rather than devising a strategy of collective responsibility and borrower empowerment, as originally envisaged by the bank. Under such pressure, many women borrowers maintain their regular repayment schedules through loan recycling which ultimately increases the debt liability of the borrower. The increased debt liability, in turn, aggravates family tension and produces new forms social dominance and often violence against women borrowers.

Empirical studies reveal that it is not always the poorest of poor women who get the credit. Those with sizeable income and assets often corner the biggest chunk of credit. Further studies have also reported that much of the credit is used by poor women to meet consumption needs rather than investment in businesses. The growing dependence of micro credit institutions on donors is a matter for serious concern. There are very few instances where micro credit institutions have become sustainable without the support of donors. This is despite the fact that most micro lenders charge relatively higher interest rates in the range of 12 to 36 per cent. Therefore, a proper regulatory framework under which micro-lenders should function is needed in India.

Women Entrepreneurs

Advocates of micro credit programmes view poverty as a cash flow problem and seek its solutions through credit and income generation programmes. Poverty particularly that of women, cannot be defined only in terms of cash flow since it has strong linkages with imaginable distribution of resources, unequal power relations, illiteracy, lower wages, cuts in developmental spending and anti-poor macro-economic policies that disproportionably affect poor women. It also needs to be emphasized that micro credit is not a substitute for social sector spending and anti poverty programmes.

In the rural context, women's control over ownership of land can play an important role not only in economic betterment but also in terms of social and political empowerment as land is a symbol of political power and social status. Further micro credit programmes have to be visualized in the context of the new global economic order in liberalization, privatisation and globalisation policies which have led to job losses in the formal sector, decline in social sector spending and growing unemployment. In this scenario, the last option left for poor women is self-employment, which micro credit aims to promote.

But poor women are placed at a disadvantageous position in the market. How can the products of poor women compete with those of big business and transactional corporations which not only have strong financial backing but also spend millions on advertising, brand-selling and marketing. Until and unless poor women are provided access to market information, technology, management and marketing skills, their economic ventures will remain uncompetitive.

Conclusion

Since the efficacy of micro credit programmes is not independent of other developmental interventions, it could at best be one of the components of a wider developmental agenda.

Women in Dairy Cooperatives

Dr. S. Eswaramoorthi

Introduction

Once, in the demand distant past, women were kept indoors and men were the sole bread winners of their families. But now, women come out of the household drudge and work on par with men and lend support to their respective. This trend is common in both urban and rural areas. Rural women take dairy activities as their main occupation in villages. They become efficient entrepreneurs to get the maximum returns for their investments. Dairy cooperatives help the women to achieve their objective. In India, women were treated as weaker sex of the society. This unsung and unutilised force is now mostly used in rural areas to increase the economic conditions of the country.

Women and Dairy Industry

Women and dairy industries are closely inter-related. They actively engage each other not only in agriculture but also in its allied activities. They carry the work with or without men for their livelihood. Dairy operations are carried more by women than men. Moreover Agriculture provides employment to them only for 90 to 120 days in a year. In the rest of the year they are idle. In this situation, women try another work which provides regular employment and income in rural areas. They see more such opportunities in dairying.

Women engage dairy activity easily because it is an agriculture related activity. Besides, they may not go out of their village to get employment elsewhere. Milk production is done by women with other domestic work.

Women get up early morning and clean the cattle shed for good sanitation. Cattle rearing, watering, exercising, providing medicines, milking are some of the dairy activities undertaken by women. They treat their milch animals as "Goddess". They manage and maintain their animals in a good manner. It is the women who know the various types of fodder and browse that can be fed to the milch animals. The disease affected animals are treated patiently by them. It is known that 90 per cent of marginal workers in rural women choose the dairying as their full time work in most parts of our country.

Role of Women in Dairy Cooperatives

At present, private dairies and milk cooperatives render immense service to the dairy-women for the enhancement of milk production. Both of them procure milk from the producers in rural areas and supply it to the urban areas. Private dairy entrepreneur's aim is to get maximum return from their investments. They are least concerned about productivity and quality. The milk producers who supply milk to the private dairies are always exploited. Low procurement price, less regular procurement, more settlement time, inconvenient procurement time and other fraudulent practices force the women to find other alternative.

In order to get relieved from the clutches of greedy private dairies, dairy cooperatives are formed in rural areas. For availing, the most benefit from the dairy activities, the women prefer to establish women milk cooperatives. Such cooperatives prevent silent, soft spoken, socially oppressed women from private dairies.

The world reputed Operation Flood programme, which we heralded as white revolution in India, also emphasized inclusion of more women members in mixed gender society and establish more milk cooperatives exclusively for women. This is due to the fact that:

(i) Women undertake dairy activities as yet another house hold work.

(ii) Women manage milk production and marketing easily as they are allied to agriculture.

(iii) Women are capable of managing this tiny units effectively.

(iv) As dairying is done at small level, this is more suitable economic activity for women to generate additional income.

Women dairy cooperatives comprise of women members form and registered under Cooperative Societies Act. It has been formed for self-help and mutual help. Now-a-days NGO's are playing a leading role in integrating the women milk producers.

To become a member in milk cooperative society, each individual has to contribute a small amount as his or her share capital for meeting the legal requirement.

Presently 6,000 out of 70,000 primary milk producers cooperative societies are women societies in India. Out of 86,66,660 total members in rural milk cooperatives 14,28,709 members are women. The percentage of women members in milk societies was about 14 a decade ago. But, it has increased to 17 per cent now.

Table 8.1 indicates the women members in Operation Flood Cooperatives.

Table 8.1 reveals that around 16.49 per cent of the total members are women. It is very low due to illiteracy, lack of awareness, lack of activeness etc. In western region, Gujarat stands first followed by Goa in having more female milk cooperative societies. In southern region Pondichery state has more percentage of women members compared with other states. In northern and eastern region Himachal Pradesh and Bihar stands first in their respective regions.

After becoming the member, the society provides the necessary financial assistance to buy high yield milch animals. Members are given sufficient training to maintain milch

Table 8.1. Women Members in Operation Flood Cooperatives 1993-94 (Final Phase)

State	All Members	Women Members	Total Members	Percentage of Women Members to Total
Western Region				
Goa	14,173	2,150	16,323	13.17
Gujarat	17,96,244	3,10,179	21,06,423	14.73
Madhya Pradesh	2,02,064	7,160	2,09,224	3.42
Maharastra	10,27,245	71,541	10,98,786	6.51
Total	**30,39,726**	**3,91,030**	**34,30,756**	**11.40**
Southern Region				
Andhra Pradesh	6,75,102	1,05,327	7,80,429	13.50
Karnataka	12,38,177	1,99,996	14,38,173	13.91
Kerala	3,06,807	37,210	3,44,017	10.82
Pondichery	18,540	6,319	24,859	25.42
Tamil Nadu	18,40,186	5,46,579	23,86,765	22.90
Total	**40,78,812**	**8,95,431**	**49,74,243**	**18.00**
Northern Region				
Haryana	1,51,839	3,793	1,55,632	2.44
Himachal Pradesh	14,073	3,038	17,111	17.75
Jammu & Kashmir	4,350	11	4,361	00.25
Punjab	3,17,615	25,146	3,42,761	07.34
Rajasthan	3,53,901	35,183	3,89,084	09.04
Uttar Pradesh	4,49,748	47,495	4,97,243	09.55
Total	**12,91,526**	**1,14,666**	**14,06,192**	**08.15**
Eastern Region				
Assam	2,174	99	2,273	4.36
Bihar	1,15,611	15,257	1,30,868	11.66
Nagaland	691	62	753	8.23
Orissa	60,533	5,950	66,483	8.23
Sikim	4,270	515	4,785	10.76
Tripura	4,070	230	4,300	5.35
West Bengal	69,247	5,469	74,716	7.32
Total	**2,56,596**	**27,582**	**2,84,178**	**9.71**
Grand Total	**86,66,660**	**14,28,709**	**1,00,95,369**	**16.49**

Source: Dairy India 1997. p. 184.

animal by experienced veterinary doctors. The milk cooperatives render services like artificial insemination, first aid, de worming, free vaccination, supply of quality feed and fodder for animals good health and enhancement of milk production. In addition to this, members benefit provident fund, thrift-habit, community services, housing facility and subsidy from the society.

Members are paid higher price than private dairies. The society procure milk regularly at the society premises/and or at the door steps of members. It is observed that the women members of the society are enjoying better standard of living as they get regular additional income by way of selling milk to the society. This economic empowerment of women give them better social status in the society which was denied to them in earlier days. They are now empowered to take economic decisions independently. Moreover, they need not depend on money-lenders as they could meet expenses from their self-generated incomes.

The milk cooperatives provide community services like road paving, providing good drinking water, running schools etc for the public in the villages.

District milk producers union at District Level, State Level federation and National Level Dairy organisation regulate the societies, supply production and technical inputs and other financial support to develop the women dairy cooperatives.

Women dairy cooperatives are proved to be successful than the ones run by their opposite sex. It is so because women are less political, self-thinking, duty conscious, sincere and committed in making their work successful.

The cooperatives create good leaders. The members elect their representatives to manage the society. They plan, organize, direct, control, motivate, lead and coordinate the society activities. Now women occupy important positions like chief executives, managers, secretary and other top level officers in dairy cooperatives. In such a way, women are empowered to have gender equality.

Conclusion

By organizing women dairy cooperatives, the rural women come out strongly from their household drudgery, poverty, ill health, illiteracy and dependability. As the dairy is closely connected with women, they get full employment and regular income throughout the year through dairying. The unutilized women sector is employed to enhance the national income and per capita income of our country. Hence organizing more number of women members dairy societies in rural areas will go a long way to achieve the desired goal of economic independence, regular source of employment and gender equality for the women in the society.

Role of Women Entrepreneurs in Societal Upliftment

Mrs. J. Jayalatha

Introduction

Today our government is more concerned about the overall economic development of women and for this, development of "Entrepreneurship" among women has become an important aspect of plan priorities. Women constitute around half of the total world population so is in India too. They are therefore, regarded as the better half of the society. In traditional societies, they were confined to the four walls of houses performing household activities. In modern societies they have come out of the four walls to participate in all sorts of activities. The global evidences prove that women have been performing exceedingly well in different spheres of activities women entry into business is a recent phenomenon. It is traced out as an extension of their kitchen activities to 3 Ps., i.e., pickles, powder (masala) and pappad manufacturing with growing awareness and spread of education over the years women have started engrossing to modern activities like engineering, electronics and energy popularly known as 3 Es.

Women Entrepreneurship

An entrepreneur is a person who has an enterprising quality with an eye on opportunities and an uncanny vision.

Commercial acumen and above all a person who is willing to take risks because of the adventurous spirit within. Same holds good for women also. The Government of India has defined women entrepreneurs based on women participation in equity and employment of a business enterprise. Accordingly a women entrepreneur is defines as "an enterprise owned and controlled by a women having a minimum financial interest of 51 per cent of the capital and giving at least 51 per cent of the employment generated in the enterprise to women".

Present Scenario

Now the scenario is fast changing with modernisation, urbanisation and development of education and business. Thus the opportunities of employment for women have increased drastically. It is found that the percentage of unemployment among educated and qualified women is increasing. Thus it is necessary to increasing the opportunity of self-employment for educated unemployed women through the development of entrepreneurship. It should be stated here that the self-employed entrepreneur creates not only her employment but also creates employment opportunities to others. It is most important to create a favourable atmosphere for a healthy development of entrepreneurship.

Problems Faced by Women Entrepreneurs

The problems faced by women entrepreneurs in the country emanate from a multitude of sources and are manifold. Entrepreneurship is not a "bed of roses" to the women. Their task has become more tedious and full of challenges since they have to encounter public prejudices and criticism. Women face certain problems not as a entrepreneur but as a woman. Therefore, when compared to men the problems of women entrepreneurs are more in number.

Problems faced by women entrepreneurs were classified as under:

1. Socio-personal problems
2. Managerial problems
3. Production problems

4. Marketing problems
5. Financial problems
6. Problems of Government Assistance

1. *Socio-personal Problems*

Most of the women are facing the problem of wrong attitude of the society against them. In a male dominated society, women are encountered with many socio-personal problems like lack of family and community support, male dominated society, lack of education and information, economic backwardness and low risk bearing capacity.

2. *Managerial Problems*

Managerial problems are another important problems faced by women entrepreneurs which are in the form of lack of knowledge of general management and experience, lack of skilled labour absenteeism and labour turnover, lack of clear cut objectives and transportation problem as women.

3. *Production Problems*

These problems are encountered by the women entrepreneurs during production process. These problems can be any of the following:

(a) Inadequate availability of land, plots and premises;

(b) Problem of getting required inputs;

(c) Inadequate Technical Support of production indentification and machinery utilisation;

(d) Lack of Upgradation of Technology, Research and Development and Quality Control;

(e) Poor Inventory Management.

4. *Marketing Problems*

Now-a-days marketing problem is common to all entrepreneurs. Most of them find it difficult to market their products. They do not posses the knowledge of how to market their products and whom to contact for the purpose. As women they face these marketing problems still more. They can be classified as:

(a) Lack of knowledge of how to market the product and whom to contact;

(b) Heavy competition with big enterprises;

(c) Exploitation by middlemen and difficulties in collection of dues;

(d) Inadequate sales promotion avenues;

(e) Lack of export marketing support.

5. ***Financial Problems***

Financial problem is a major problem faced by all entrepreneurs. Finance is essential to start as well as to run a business enterprise. Most of the women entrepreneurs are facing financial problems at the time of starting as well as during operation of their business enterprises. The financial problems take the shape of:

(a) Problem of getting loan and subsidy;

(b) Insistence or collateral and margin money requirement;

(c) Time taken to process loan;

(d) Tight repayment schedule;

(e) Poor Financial Management and maintenance of accounts.

6. ***Problems of Government Assistance***

Both Central and State Governments are implementing various assistance schemes for promotion of women entrepreneurship. But in practice women entrepreneurs are facing many difficulties in obtaining various government of assistance. They are:

(a) Inadequate Government assistance;

(b) Red-tapism of various levels;

(c) Advisory organisations become explotive and dishonest;

(*d*) Complicated and time consuming procedures for getting the assistance;

(*e*) Government policies are not favourable.

Mode of Assistance

To widen and strengthen the base of women entrepreneurship the following remedial measures may prove meaningful:

1. Governmental financial institution should implement to solve financial problems, and implement special lending polices, quick processing of loan and liberal repayment schedule for women entrepreneurs;
2. The Government should give subsidies and concessions to women entrepreneurs to face price competition from big enterprises. Government and women entrepreneurs association should make arrangement for conducting exhibitions and conferences of women entrepreneurs;
3. Attention of the government should be drawn in rectifying the production problems by the allotment of factory shed and land in government industrial estates on priority basis, supply of raw materials and other inputs regularly at subsidised rates, giving assistance for upgradation of technology research and development and giving production training to women entrepreneurs;
4. Attention of the government as well as voluntary organisations need to be drawn to rectify socio-personal problems. A special programme can be conducted against the social evils.

Adequate assistance should be given to the right person at the right time. A special advisory organisation should be established. Simplified procedures should be followed in getting the government assistance.

Conclusion

The growth of industrialisation, education and domestic system has brought about significant changes in the tradition bound Indian society. Now increasing proportion of women are seeking gainful employment in industrial field. It is a fact that man alone cannot break the evils of poverty, unemployment and inequality. Active and equal participation of women is indispensable in fighting against this social evils.

Socio-economic Constraints of Rural Women Entrepreneurs

Dr. K. Ramamoorthy
Mr. S. Ramesh Kumar

Introduction

Indian women are considered as source of power (Shakti) since mythological times. Goddesses are being worshipped as mother in the major religions of India, which means the mother is the source, giving life to everyone. Moreover the mother is the first teacher for the young ones, who helps to recognize the world from the beginning.

At the same time, in the sociological setup, the Indian society is a male dominant one. Women are considered as weaker sex and are left with closed commitments only. Such sociological and cultural habits, have been keeping the women sector of the Indian population, a dormant one for quite a long time.

Indian women are patient in nature and do have the capacity to accept things, normally they do have more confidence on the male members of the family. Our culture makes them good subordinates and executors of the decisions made by the male members. In general women folk are capable of working hard physically on all occasions and mostly at all stages, with these built up characteristics and infrastructure in which they live, the entrepreneurship of the Indian women is to be looked into.

But now the scenario is changing fast with modernisation, urbanisation and development of education and business. Women are now seeking gainful employment in several fields in increasing numbers with the spread of education and new awareness.

A family is the nucleus of the society, similarly an entrepreneur is the nucleus of the economy. *"When women move forward the family moves, the village moves, and the nation moves"*. These words of Jawaharlal Nehru are often repeated because it is an accepted fact.

Rural women force remains an unorganized one. Young and middle-aged group will be the major constituents in this sector. Women in rural areas and economically weaker sections are engaged in farm labour and get their daily earnings. Women from middle class and upper middle class are themselves included in income earning activities at their own level. Such rural women are involved in money-lending, though making with wet grinders, papad and pickles making, dairy products production, maintenance of poultry, vadam and other eatable products making and selling at their level, many illiterate women are also involved in it.

Employment: Employment gives economic status to women. Economic status paves way for social status. Women constitute almost half of the population. In the rural sector almost 56 per cent of the males and 33 per cent of the females were in the labour force during 1999. About 66 per cent of the female population in the rural sector is idle and unutilized. This is mainly due to existing social customs. The young girls and women are not allowed to work independently.

Self-employment is the safe way to generate income. Economic development is barred on the high individual income. In addition, self-employment also changes the position of women from being job seeker to job givers. The quest for economic independence and better social status and sometimes sheer need of the family's survival, force women to self-employment and entrepreneurship (Pillai and Anna, 1990). The role of women entrepreneurs helps industrial development, promotes economic development and helps to solve the problems of unemployment and poverty. However women in business is a recent phenomenon in India. Emergence of women entrepreneurs in the economy is an indicator of women's economic independence and their improved social status.

Many studies have proved that unemployment and poverty are contributing factors for the emergence of women entrepreneurs. Besides in rural areas self-employment helps to solve unemployment and to generate additional incomes through activities like tailoring, agarbatti manufacturing, papad making, embroidery, pickle manufacturing, small retail shops and fruit canning.

Rural Women Entrepreneurs

Entrepreneurs play a key role in the economic development of a country. Entrepreneurship may be regarded as a powerful tool for economic development of a predominating agricultural economy like India.

Enterprise: An enterprise is the basic unit of an economic organization that transacts with other units in the economy and produces products and services with more than the value of resources used.

Entrepreneur: The term 'entrepreneur' taken from the old French word "entrepreneuriat" meaning "to undertake" the term entrepreneur refers to "one who organises, operates and assumes the risk of business venture".

Women Entrepreneur: Women entrepreneurs are defined as "the women or group of women who initiate, organize and operate a business enterprise".

Government of India defines women entrepreneur as "an enterprise owned and controlled by a woman and having a minimum financial interest of 51 per cent of the capital and giving at least 51 per cent of employment to women".

Rural Women Entrepreneur

"A rural woman entrepreneur is a woman or group of women who undertake to organize and run an enterprise in a rural area".

Rural women become entrepreneur due to several factors, which may be grouped under "pull factors" and "push factors". *Pull factors* refer to the urge in women to undertake a venture with an inclination to start a business. *Push factors* refer to women entering business driven by financial need due to family circumstances are said to be influenced by push factors.

Constraints to Rural Women Entrepreneurs

The role of women in productive activities in India has been increasing over the years, however, the total number of enterprises run by them is insignificantly small. The number of enterprises initiated and being run by women in the formal sector is small.

Rural women are more vulnerable in comparison to urban women, because the urban women have wide scope of activities around them to explore but rural women do not get enough opportunity to make use of their economic potential.

Though women are equally qualified as men to succeed as entrepreneurs, they suffer from different types of constraints. The women entrepreneurs face additional hurdles than those of men. As Kamla Singh (1992) put it they face constraints relating to self-sphere system, which consists of age, experience, education, knowledge etc, Socio-sphere system, which consists of entrepreneurial motivation, job satisfaction, value orientation, decision making ability, family occupation-caste etc.

The other hurdles which the rural women entrepreneurs face are related to:

- Cultural barriers
- Educational barriers
- Political barriers

- Technological barriers, and
- Legislative protective measures.

The important problems faced by the rural women entrepreneurs are classified into different categories, viz.,

- Socio-personal problems
- Managerial problems
- Production problems
- Marketing problems
- Financial problems, and
- Problems of Government Assistance.

Social Constraints of Rural Women Entrepreneurs

1. Men have negative attitudes towards female, therefore gender discrimination is prevailing. Due to family responsibilities rural women entrepreneurs have less time compared to males they have to look after both their family and business.
2. Women entrepreneurs in rural areas have to face not only resistance and reservation from men but also from elderly women who are imprisoned in the attitude of inequality.
3. The ability and different types of skills possed by the rural women entrepreneurs is not recognized by the society, because of the society's lack of confidence in women's ability.
4. The family's reluctance to finance and to take risks on projects set up by women entrepreneurs in rural areas is the main reason for the lack of growth in their venture.
5. A woman entrepreneur should consider her family background, education, attitude and skill she has acquired. She cannot venture totally in new area, because of the wrong attitude towards the rural women entrepreneurs by the society and the term lending financial institutions.

6. The women entrepreneurs in rural areas are facing stiff competition from their male counterparts in terms of production and marketing of their products and services.

7. Women by their very nature are less mobile and they are deprived of low cost and high efficiency. The socio-cultural background binds them.

8. Women are generally conservative and so do not dare to undertake risk. Fear of loss and inferiority complex also deter them from taking risks. So women normally prefer traditional areas, which are less risky such as tailoring, embroidery, pickle making, fruit canning and handicrafts.

Financial Constraints of Rural Women Entrepreneur

Finance means more than merely obtaining money, it is very much a process of managing assets wisely to use capital efficiency.

Finance is essential to start as well as to run a business enterprise. Most of the rural women entrepreneurs are facing financing problems at the time of starting as well as during operation of their business enterprises. The following are the important financial constraints faced by the rural women entrepreneurs:

1. Rural women entrepreneurs are handicapped by lack of adequate finance, technical know-how, non-availability of raw materials, lack of technical and managerial skills;

2. After the amendment of the relevant act women have been endowed with equal share in the family properties. But it is not followed in practice;

3. Procedures of bank loans and delay and the running about deter many women from venturing;

4. At government level licensing authorities, labour officers and sales tax inspectors put all sorts of humiliating questions;

5. Since most of the rural women entrepreneurs do not enjoy legal right over property of any form, they have limited, access over external sources of funds. Even the family members have no confidence in the capacity of women in running the business;

6. Institution and commercial banks do not come forward to lend loan to women members who are basically housewives with less exposure to business and risk;

7. The important constraints faced by the rural women entrepreneurs is that the time taken by the banks and financial institution to process the loan and also compliant the tight repayment schedule given by the term lending institutions;

8. Poor education and lack of exposure in financial management practices and maintenance of accounts leads to improper planning and development in their business.

Conclusion

The rural women entrepreneurs are taking up challenging entrepreneurial activities. In rural areas larger amount of potential, remain untapped due to lack of supportive means and management. The constraint they face is basically related to finance, which must be removed by attending, immediately by authorities concerned. Proper entrepreneurial skill and marketing talent are to be given to the rural women entrepreneurs through proper training programmes for carrying entrepreneurial activities. If they are given proper education and awareness about entrepreneurial activities they will become an important source for the economic development of our nation.

References

1. W. Haynes, *"Principles of Management and Entrepreneurship Development"*- New Central Book Agency (P) Ltd., Calcutta-700 009, 1999. pp. 15, 16, 148.

2. M. Sundra Pandian, *"Women Entrepreneurship Issues and Strategies"*- Kanishka Publishers, Distributors, New Delhi-110 002, 1999.

3. J.V. Prabakara Rao, *"Entrepreneurship and Economic Development"* Kanishka Publishers, Distributors, New Delhi—110 002, 2000.

4. I.C. Dhingra, V.K. Garg, *"Economics for ICWA. Foundation Course:-* Sultan Chand & Sons, New Delhi—110 002, 1995. pp. 133-134.

5. Amitabha Mukherjee, *"How Entrepreneurs Shape the Economy"*- Management Accountant, vol. No: 33, No: 7, July 1998, p. 554.

6. R. Hiremani Naik *"Problems of Women Entrepreneurs - A Pilor Study"*, Southern Economist, Vol. No: 40, Nov. 1, 2001. pp. 17-18.

Micro Enterprises and Rural Women

Dr. Punithavathy Pandian
R. Eswaran

Entrepreneur is a highly respected 'word' in the developed world. It conjures up visions of active, purposeful men and women accomplishing a wide variety of significant deeds. Entrepreneurs is one of the most enigmatic characters in the drama of economic development, particularly in the less developed world.[1] In India, entrepreneurial world is men's world predominantly. But recently, there is a change in the trend. It has been increasingly realised that enterprising women have vast entrepreneurial talents which could be harnessed so as to convert them from the position of 'Job Seekers' to 'Job Giver'.

The status of women is closely associated with their economic position, which in turn, depends upon their access to productive resources of the country and the opportunities for participation in economic activities.[2] Economic independence of women with equal opportunity brings out their full potentials as human beings instead of being considered appendages to males.[3] Women's skill and knowledge, their talents and abilities in business and a compelling desire of wanting to do something positive are some of the reasons for the women entrepreneurs to organise enterprises. In rural areas, several NGOs are working on poverty alleviation and income generating activities among rural poor by instilling the concept of women entrepreneurship. The NGOs develop management skill at the grassroot level. They help them to utilise the indigenous knowledge of management. NGOs with the help of the Self Help Groups reach out the rural women.

SHGs are of recent origin in India. Self Help Groups (SHGs) are small, economically homogeneous and affinity groups of rural/urban poor women, voluntarily formed to save and contribute to a common fund to be lent to its members as per group decision and for working together for social and economic uplift of their families and community.[4] These groups organise rural poor women and motivate entrepreneurship in them by providing financial help in a small way under micro-credit scheme.

Micro-credit programmes extent small loans to poor people for self-employment projects that generate income allowing them to care for themselves and their families. In most cases, micro-credit programmes offer a combination of services and resources to their clients in addition to credit for self-employment. These often include savings facilities, training, networking, and peer support.

Several studies have been conducted on entrepreneurship related to large, medium and small scale industries. But, the micro entrepreneurs are the neglected lot. Hence, this paper has been devoted to study the micro entrepreneurs whom we meet often in our day to day life.

Data

A sample of 350 women from ten sample blocks of Madurai District wherein the NGOs are working has been chosen at random for the purpose of this study. These sample women have been identified by CRED, ICCW, SHEPHERD, SEWA, and ASSEFA as individuals in the beginning to start with, guided to form a group to mobilise small savings and later are facilitated to avail credit from the Commercial Banks, Regional Rural Banks and Co-operative Banks. Now, these women are the members of the bank and they are extended with credit on successful identification of a micro enterprise. Primary data were collected with the help of structured interview schedules from the sample women entrepreneurs.

Micro Enterprises and Rural Women

The sample women respondent who run micro enterprises are referred to as entrepreneurs in this study. The sample micro enterprises are categorised into petty business, processing, production units and service units. The petty business consists of tiffin centers, tea stall, retailing of milk, vegetables, cloth and ready-made garments. The processing units are mainly concerned with masala powder and pickle making. The production units are mainly furniture making, basket making and mat making. Service units are of tailoring shops.

Table 11.1. Distribution of the Sample Respondents by Nature of Business

Sl. No.	Nature of the Business Undertaken	Number of Women Entrepreneurs	Percentage to Total
1.	Petty Business Units	181	51.71
2.	Processing Units	41	11.71
3.	Production Units	58	16.57
4.	Service Units	70	20.00
	Total	**350**	**100.00**

Source: Primary Data.

It is found that majority of the women (52%) belong to petty business units and the remaining are distributed among processing, production and service units.

Micro Enterprises and Extent of Borrowing

In order to find out the relationship between the nature of micro enterprises and extent of borrowing, the entrepreneurs are categorised into three groups namely, entrepreneurs who have undertaken petty business, processing, and production, and service units. Table 11.2

shows the nature of micro enterprises undertaken by them and extent of borrowing under micro-credit scheme.

Table 11.2. Nature of Micro Enterprises and Extent of Borrowing

Nature of Micro Enterprises	Extent of Borrowing		Percentage to Total
	Below Rs. 2500	Rs. 2500 and above	
Petty Business	123 (68.00)	58 (32.00)	181 (100.00)
Processing and Production Units	31 (31.00)	68 (69.00)	99 (100.00)
Service Units	19 (27.00)	51 (73.00)	70 (100.00)
Total	**173**	**177**	**350**

Source: Primary Data.

(Figures in brackets are percentages to total)

In the petty business units, 68 per cent of the sample women entrepreneurs have borrowed below Rs. 2500 whereas only 32 per cent of the sample women entrepreneurs have borrowed above Rs. 2500. In the service units, 73 per cent of the sample women entrepreneurs have borrowed above Rs. 2500 whereas only 27 per cent of the sample women entrepreneurs have borrowed below Rs. 2500.

The chi-square test had been applied to find out the relationship between borrowings and the nature of enterprises and the result is given below:

Hypotheses

H_0 : Nature of micro enterprises does not influence the level of borrowing.

H_1 : Nature of micro enterprises influences the level of borrowing

Calculated value of χ^2= 52.38

Degrees of freedom = 1

Table value of χ^2 test at 5 per cent level of significance = 3.841

The calculated chi-square value is greater than the table value of χ^2 at 5 per cent level of significance hence, the null hypothesis is rejected. Therefore, there is a relationship between the nature of micro enterprises and the extent of borrowing.

Majority of the women entrepreneurs those who are doing petty business have borrowed below Rs. 2500. But, those who engaged in service and production units have borrowed above Rs. 2500. This might be due to the higher requirements of funds to install service units. Thus, it is concluded from the above analysis that the nature of micro enterprises by the entrepreneurs have influenced the extent of borrowings of the sample women entrepreneurs.

Micro Entrepreneurs and Literacy Level

The social aspect of human life is maintained and transmitted by education. Education can be related to all spheres of economic activities such as consumption, investment, employment, human resource development and the like. The educated entrepreneurs can wisely plan their business and avoid unnecessary expenditure. Education creates better understanding and increases the efficiency. It would also develop entrepreneurs aptitude, initiative and interest in the business. To find out whether there is an association between level of education and nature of micro enterprises, a two-way table is prepared. The sample women entrepreneurs are divided into two groups namely literate and illiterates.

Table 11.3. Level of Literacy and Nature of Micro Enterprises

Level of Literacy	Petty Business	Processing and Production	Service	Total	Percentage to Total
Illiterate	69	14	13	96	27.43
Literate	112	85	57	254	72.57
Total	**181**	**99**	**70**	**350**	**100.00**

Source: Primary Data.

It could be noted that illiterates form 27.43 per cent. On the whole more than 72 per cent of the enterprises are run by women with certain level of literacy attainment. High percentage of illiterate women are engaged in petty business compared to the literate women. More literate women are engaged in processing, production and service units.

Chi-square test had been applied to find out the relationship between the entrepreneurs literacy level and the nature of micro enterprises.

Hypotheses

H_0 : Literacy level of the micro entrepreneurs does not influence the nature of enterprises.

H_1 : Literacy level of the micro entrepreneurs influences the nature of enterprises

Calculated value of χ^2= 21.19

Degrees of freedom = 2

Table value of χ^2 test at 5 per cent level of significance = 5.991.

Since the calculated χ^2 value is greater than the table value, the null hypothesis is rejected. Literacy influences the nature of enterprises. The literate women take up processing, production units with more confidence. The educated and the uneducated suffer due to lack of employment. Unemployment pushes them into the viscous circle of poverty. Everybody in the society tries to get employment in their own way.

Reasons for Starting Units

The reasons for starting the micro enterprises of sample women entrepreneurs are given in Table 11.4.

It is learnt that majority has been motivated to be self employed and 35 per cent of them have started enterprises for the training received on similar grounds and few of them have entered into the micro enterprises to earn money. Hence, the present study indicates a departure from the accepted fact that the need to achieve and the ability to take calculated risk are the prime factors for the people to enter into a business. It may be true for large-scale, high-tech industries where it is quite challenging and risky to compete with similar units run by their male counterparts. But the nature of business undertaken by the entrepreneurs in this study is mainly related to self employment.

Table 11.4. Reasons behind Starting Micro Enterprises

Factor	Petty Business	Processing	Production	Service	Total	Percentage to Total
To be Self Employed	88	14	8	13	123	35.14
To earn Money	33	7	14	13	67	19.14
Trained	36	14	27	37	114	32.57
Family Business	24	6	9	7	46	13.14
Total	**181**	**41**	**58**	**70**	**350**	**100.00**

Source: Primary Data.

Age-wise Distribution of Entrepreneurs

It is a commonly held belief that as an individual grows up in age he/she tends to mature in wisdom and experience. With maturity and vast experience, entrepreneurs at the higher age group can achieve goals expected of their performance with greater ease and intelligence. Age of the sample entrepreneurs and the nature of micro enterprises are given in Table 11.5.

Table 11.5. Age-wise Distribution of Sample Entrepreneurs

Age in Years	Petty Business	Processing	Production	Service	Total	Percentage to Total
20-30	42	9	12	13	76	21.71
30-40	56	13	25	27	121	34.57
40-50	52	11	14	19	96	27.43
Above 50	31	8	7	11	57	16.29
Total	**181**	**41**	**58**	**70**	**350**	**100.00**

Source: Primary Data.

The age-wise distribution explains that the sample entrepreneurs in petty business, processing, production and service units are relatively young being in the age group of 30-40. Most of the women in this age group are married. This proves that more married women enter into business than unmarried women in spite of their duel role in the society. Experience and age have been a determining factor of entrepreneurship.

Community-wise Distribution of Entrepreneurs

Caste system prevails in India from time immemorial. The economically and socially backward classes remained and served the richer communities in the traditional society. The Table 11.6 attempts to show the micro enterprises and the social groups.

Table 11.6. Community-wise Distribution of Sample Entrepreneurs

Community	Petty Business	Processing	Production	Service	Total	Percentage to Total
S.C.	51	8	12	17	88	25.14
M.B.C.	46	11	16	21	94	26.86
B.C.	77	21	28	30	156	44.57
O.C.	7	1	2	2	12	3.43
Total	**181**	**41**	**58**	**70**	**350**	**100.00**

Source: Primary Data.

The community-wise distribution tells that economically and socially weaker sections have also taken up entrepreneurial activities as 45 per cent of them belong to BCs. One fourth of the sample belongs to SC. It is heartening to note that these groups are becoming managers of micro enterprises, which is really a breakthrough.

Employment

Most of the rural women are underemployed and unemployed. Their potentials remain underutilised and unexploited in many cases. The pre-employment details of the micro entrepreneurs are given below in Table 11.7.

Table 11.7. Pre-loan Employment Details of the Micro Entrepreneurs

Details of Pre-loan Occupation	Total Entrepreneurs	Percentage to Total
Underemployed	237	67.71
Unemployed	113	32.29
Total	**350**	**100.00**

Source: Primary Data.

Table 11.7 indicates that their vast potential remain unutilised and they suffered due to lack of employment. After starting the enterprises all of them are employed. They also created employment opportunities for their idle family members. Most of the processing and production unit employ their own family members.

Conclusion

The micro entrepreneurs are the new stream of entrepreneurs who help to solve the problem of rural poverty. Creation of self employment and earning a livelihood make them to venture into micro enterprises. The success of these micro entrepreneurs depend on the further support system, the society and the Government are willing to provide for them.

References

1. G. Wayne, Jr. Brochl, The Village Entrepreneur, (London: Harward University Press, 1978), p. 1.
2. Chetana, Kalpagh, Women and Development Women Employment and the Work Place, Vol. 1, (New Delhi: Discovery Publishing House, 1991), pp. 1-15.
3. "Working Women Must Fight Against Social Injustice", Express News Service, *Indian Express,* August 13, 1994, p. 5.
4. "The SHGs Experience—An Introduction", Credit Guidelines for SHGs, Tamil Nadu Corporation for Development of Women Limited, p. 1.
5. *Ibid.*, p. 3.

Self Help Groups in Rural Women Entrepreneurism

A. Lakshmi

Our nation is agro-centred and hence majority of masses are tend to depend upon agriculture. It is roughly estimated 65 per cent of the masses depend on agriculture. Dr. Gro Harlem Brundtland, the first woman Director General of World Health Organisation assessed that there are 900 million illiterate people globally (30 crores in India). Illiteracy is a debility and unless methods to eradicate this malady are taken the process of rural transformation will not be a success. Unless the success of the process of rural transformation is attained, social and material advancement for majority of the people will not be possible. Hence the economy will tumble down.

People's participation in the development process is a major factor in determining the destiny of the people of rural area. Our society is unequal. Rich and powerful echelons of the society take a major share of benefits and the majority of the society (i.e.) poor section has always been deprived and marginalised. One such common ills in our society is that women are exploited while their labour are utilised for livelihood. Many of the working women in rural areas are dynamic in nature and their participation in rural employment is considerably significant. Entrepreneurial skills in their day to day working are put to use but their economic status has not improved.

Between 1971 and 1981 the overall work participation rate for females is 12.06 per cent in 1971, increased to 13.99 per cent in 1981. This necessitated their looking for financial credit from the banks and other financial institutions. But due to procedural tangle, extraction of high rate of interest by money-lenders and due to off shoot of illiteracy they are unable to be dependent upon these banks and financial institutions for their credit.

Alternatively, Self Help Groups sprouted and they form a viable alternative in the matter of getting financial assistance. Self Help Group is a voluntary group valuing personal interaction and mutual aid as means of altering and ameliorating problems perceived as alterable, pressing and personal by most of its participants who are its members. It may be noticeably noted that for the first time a work group on women employment was constituted by the Planning Commission in the Sixth Plan (1980-1985).

The Researcher makes an attempt to deal with how Self Help Group (SHG) develops rural women Entrepreneurism and the linkage of banks and Self Help Group benefit and various other aspects and features of Self Help Groups.

Entrepreneurial Opportunities for Women in Rural India

Dr. R.M. Nagammai

Historically, in India, it has been seen that entrepreneurship is monopolised by certain communities—the Marwaris, Baniyas, Vaishyas, etc. Ever since India gained independence one has seen the process of rapid modernisation and industrialisation. These entrepreneurial communities took advantage of these processess to consolidate their position both in business and trade. However, the consolidation process did not remain restricted to these communities. The non-traditional communities, the agriculturists too, acquired wealth. In no time they started challenging the superior position of the traditional business communities. The state of Punjab is a classic example of such a process.

In India about 50 per cent of total population constitutes women, but women workers constitute only 16 per cent of total population. Out of this 16 per cent, 80 per cent remains employed in unorganized sectors. Unless women contribute economically, the country cannot progress. The role of rural women in economic activities was brought into limelight by the world conference on "An Agrarian Reforms and Rural Development" in 1979. The conference pledged equal participation for women along with men in social, economical and political processes of rural development.

One way of alleviating poverty in India is to develop rural entrepreneurship. Nearly 80 per cent of the population live in rural India. Majority of them depend on agriculture for their livelihood which in turn depends upon the monsoon. During non-season and failure of monsoons they need an alternative source of employment/occupation. Micro-enterprises will provide them with an alternate source of income.

Micro-enterprise development programmes focus on creating jobs, increasing the economic stability of individuals and communities, alleviating poverty, and increasing economic self-sufficiency. In advance countries like USA also we found lot of importance and encouragement given to micro-enterprises. The Aspen Institute, a research organization estimates that there are more than 350 micro enterprise development programmes and at least two million low-income micro entrepreneurs in the United States. The United States has experienced tremendous growth in small businesses, especially among very small businesses started by women and minority entrepreneurs. Business owned by women now account for nearly 40 per cent of all American firms.

Entrepreneurship among women is a recent phenomenon in India. Instances of rural women being engaged in business are not many. Entrepreneurship calls for all those personal abilities and characteristics which could be developed in women folk.

Concept of Women Entrepreneurship

An entrepreneur is one who introduces something new into the economy. In Indian context, entrepreneur is more an adapter or 'initiator' than a true innovator. Therefore any woman who initiates innovations or adapts an economic activity may be called woman entrepreneur.

According to Government of India, women entrepreneur is defined as an enterprise owned and controlled by a woman and having a minimum financial interest of 51 per cent of the capital and giving at least 51 per cent of employment generated in the enterprise to women.

Reasons for the Slow Growth of Women Entrepreneurship

Women in traditional societies are still confined to four walls of home, children and family. Women are taught to depend upon others and to limit their ambitions and to avoid exposure to risks. They are under the protective wings of their better halves. Such orientation and role prescriptions inhibit the development of self-confidence, innovations, achievement, motivation and risk-taking-ability which are essential for an entrepreneur career.

Rural Women Entrepreneurship

In rural environment, the entrepreneurial ambition of women to secure independent living, to gain social prestige and self-accomplishment are not persuasive. Rural women do not aspire for independence through entrepreneurial development. It is the compelling factors like low income, unemployment and other family conditions which motivate them to start micro-enterprises. The reasons to start micro-enterprise by women are:

- To supplement family income
- To continue the traditional family occupation for income
- To become financially independent
- Forced to respond to household's increasing needs
- To improve status in the family and society

Women owned micro-enterprises have some basic characteristics, viz:

- They need small credit/loan to start business. The investment is normally upto Rs. 10000 in rural areas
- They are mostly located at home
- They use local raw materials or natural resources
- They have traditional skills and crafts
- Majority of the enterprises are seasonal in nature
- Produce simple outputs either consumer goods or intermediate goods

- The activities generally suit the life-style of women
- They are assisted by one or more family members

In case of women micro-enterprises, growth is not a major phenomenon. Women tend to limit their products and do not diversify.

Various Government Credit Schemes for Women

Some of the schemes of Government which provide credit and fund are:

- Integrated Rural Development Programme (IRDP)
- Training of Rural Youth for Self-Employment (TRYSEM)
- Prime Minister's Rojagar Yojana (PMRY)
- Women's Development Corporation Scheme (WDCS)
- Working Women's Forum
- Indira Mahila Yojana
- Indira Mahila Kendra at Anganwadi level
- Rashtriya Mahila Kosh
- Mahila Samiti Yojana
- Khadi & Village Industries Commission
- Indira Priyadarshini Yojana
- SIDBI's Mahila Udyam Nidhi Mahila Vikas Nidhi
- SBI's Sree Shakti Scheme
- NGOs Credit Schemes
- National Bank for Agriculture and Rural Development (NABARD)

has formulated schemes of rural women micro enterprise support and re-financing and it operates through NGOs and Banks.

At present the Government of India has over 27 schemes for women operated by different Departments and Ministries.

In spite of introduction of such schemes for creation of micro-enterprises for women, it is sad to note that only 5 per cent of entrepreneurs in the country are women.

Poor rural women face great difficulties in gaining access to credit. Many of the rural women do not have the skills nor the resources (literacy, basic accounting, knowledge) in order to apply for loans. Also in terms of self-confidence and self-dignity that is necessary for a person to walk into a formal sector institution and ask for a loan. Developmental NGOs play a very important role in making the women aware of the source of credit. Neighbours and friends play an important role in making women entrepreneurs aware about the source of credit/loan.

Business Opportunities for Rural Women

Depending on the demographic background, educational level, previous work experience, family occupation, etc, women in rural areas can opt for manufacturing, trading or service activities. Some of the manufacturing activities they can perform are: appalam making, bangles making, basket making, brick making, detergent soap making, herbal medicine production, paper toys making, pot making, soda making, weaving, yarn production and the like. Some of the trade they can enter into successfully are: cloth trade, fruit stall, firewood selling, small shop, provision store, vegetable stall, selling curd and ghee and the like. Some of the service areas where they can thrive are: fast food, ironing, printing, tailoring, tea shop, tiffin service, vessel suppliers and the like. Investment for such small ventures may not exceed Rs. 10,000, which they can easily get from SHGs or micro credit schemes of banks.

Role of NGOs and SHGs in the Development of Rural Women Entrepreneurs

Due to gender bias and social status, it is difficult for a poor woman to venture into any micro-enterprise individually. If they form groups, then the possibility of their success increases. The experiences of few Women Self Help Groups (WSHGs) provided beyond doubt that poor women as a group are creditworthy.

Women self-help groups are small and economically homogeneous, voluntarily formed groups to save and mutually agree to contribute to a common fund to be lent to its members. The main purpose of SHGs is to save and lend (credit) to meet domestic as well as small business/micro-enterprise needs. They linked with the banks for credit also, after the initial savings are done and groups are stable. Generally, SHGs are organised by NGOs. The NGOs main role in SHG development is to inculcate and promote thrift saving habits among the group members and link them with the bank.

To develop Women Self Help Groups, a pilot project for linking SHGs with banks was introduced in 1992 to supplement the women entrepreneurs credit needs through the banking system. NABARD is providing 100 per cent refinance assistance to banks for this purpose.

NGOs could help rural women identify the activity which will yield more revenue, as most of the activities taken up by them are traditional and have less earning potential. Through various need based short term courses like Entrepreneurship Development Courses and Technical Training Programmes, NGOs can develop self-confidence in rural and skills in rural women to take-up self-employment and income-generating activities.

Constraints of Women Entrepreneurship

Although the problems are faced equally by men and women alike, women are prone to more specific problems because of traditional role they are expected to play in the society. Inborn traits of feminity such as shyness inhibitions debilitate the enterprising spirit. It leads to lack of confidence in her. They do not have access to information as much as men have. Before marriage women are not allowed to take up entrepreneurial activities outside the family environment. Low literacy level and minimum exposure to outside practical world, add to the problem of rural women entrepreneurs.

Support Needed for Rural Women Entrepreneurs

Apart from credit, women needed support at various stages of the enterprise building and management. The support extended to women entrepreneurs can be classified into training support, family support and marketing support.

Training support: To help the rural poor-women to start income generating activities/enterprises, there are several organizations imparting business/technical training. CEDs, DICs, Banks and Women Organizations conduct training programmes.

Family support for business: In the prevailing Indian tradition women are not free to act according to their choice, especially when they want to enter in the income generating/ business activities. They have to consult their husbands and other persons of the family. Support from husband and other family members gives strength to women to venture into business.

Marketing support: Modern marketing whether it is urban areas or rural areas involves movement of the entrepreneurs. In certain economic activities the movement for marketing their products or services is easy. For example, women engaged in enterprises like, vegetables, fruit vending, papad, garment, handicraft items, sari trade, etc., are selling these products in the villages from door to door, and do not face many problems. But if they are in non-traditional enterprises like washing powder, rexin, box, bangles, stapler pins, tube light choke, etc., then movement for business is necessary and often difficult. Here only, they need the support and help from their husbands.

Strategy for Development of Women Entrepreneurship in Rural India

- Self-confidence should be developed in them by having an interaction with the successful women entrepreneurs
- Literacy level of rural women should be enhanced
- All women entrepreneurs should join and form co-operative societies to see their enterprises run effectively
- Rural women should be made aware of various credit facilities, financial incentives and subsidies. Literate

women in villages should be included in committees for credit schemes at the taluk level and district level for participatory planning

- NGOs who have direct contact and influence on rural people should play a vital role in shaping and guiding them in running an enterprise
- Government together with NGOs and financial institutions should work out need based financial schemes, and provide money to capable rural women to take up self-employment and entrepreneurial activities. There should be flexibility in targets based on needs
- GOs and NGOs should encourage participation of capable women in their training programmes on income generation self-employment. The training centres should be easily accessible to the target group.

Conclusion

Women have the potential and will to establish and manage enterprises of their own. There are greater opportunities for rural women to establish and run a micro-enterprise. Money is available under different schemes. Training programmes are being conducted on different aspects of running an enterprise. NGOs are there to help them and provide them with all necessary inputs in starting and managing an enterprise. What they need is encouragement and support from the family members, Government, societies, male counterparts. With the right assistance from varied groups, they can join the mainstream of national economy and thereby contribute to the economic growth of the country.

References

1. Colette Dumas, *Micro Enterprise Training for Low-Income Women: The Case of the Community Entrepreneurs Programme*, The Journal of Entrepreneurship, Vol. 10, No. 1, January-June, 2001.
2. Mario Rutten, *Family Enterprises and Business Partnerships: Rural Entrepreneurs in India, Malaysia, and Indonesia,* The Journal of Entrepreneurship, Vol. 10, No. 2, July-December, 2001.

3. Jubilee Navaprabha, *Development of Rural Women Entrepreneurs in India,* Indian Commerce Bulletin, Vol. 6, No. 2, December, 2002.

4. International Centre for Entrepreneurship and Career Development, *Study of Credit Flow and its Utilisation by Rural Women in Micro-Enterprises,* ICECD, Ahmedabad.

Women Entrepreneurs in the Rural India

Dr. V. Madasamy,
G. Thangapandi

Introduction

Women constitute around half of the total world population. In traditional societies, they are confined to the four walls of the houses perfuming household activities. In modern societies they have come out of the four walls to participate in all sorts of activities. They have started plunging into industry and running their enterprises successfully. They are ready to take risks, face challenges and prove to the world that their role in society is no more limited to that of buyers but can extend to that of successful sellers. Now-a-days, women have become more independent and achievement oriented.

Concept of Women Entrepreneurship

Women Entrepreneurs may be defined as the woman or a group of women who initiate, organise and operate a business enterprise, women who innovate, imitate or adopt an economic activity are called "Women Entrepreneurs". The Government of India has defined women entrepreneur based on women participation in management and employment of a business enterprise. Accordingly, an enterprise owned and controlled by women having a minimum financial interest of

51 per cent of the capital and giving at least 51 per cent of the employment, generated in the enterprise to women.

Functions of Women Entrepreneur

Now-a-days, the following are the major functions performed by women entrepreneurs in India:

- Exploring of the prospects of starting a new business enterprise
- Undertaking risk and handling of economic uncertainties
- Introduction of innovations
- Co-ordination, administration and control
- Supervision and leadership

Growth of Women Entrepreneurship in Rural Areas

In the beginning, women lacked appropriate corporate vision in fixing targets, priorities criteria and identification of appropriate beneficiaries. From 1981 onwards, the Government has started Skill Development Programme (SDP) in interior villages for women living below poverty line. By 1984, they felt that lack of proper education is one of the reasons for their poverty. Hence, the Government started Adult Education Programme (AEP) for women to create proper social environment, which was later expanded further. From 1990 onwards, the Government involved District Rural Development Agency (DRDA) to conduct TRYCEM programme for DWCRA beneficiaries. By the end of 1998-99 women formed 210 autonomous women groups. They have also started Entrepreneur development programmes exclusively for women having some educational background or skill.

Women Entrepreneurs in Rural India

Participation of women in entrepreneurial activities in India is comparatively a recent phenomenon. Figures relating to 1988-89 reveal that there are more than 1,53,260 women entrepreneurs claiming 9.01 per cent of the total 1.7 million entrepreneurs in India. But now, this has been doubled the percentage, when compared to 1988. Of this, a majority of them were in comparatively low paid and low-productivity jobs in the rural area. The present figures further reveal that only 12.4 per cent of the total self-employed women were in the organised sector. In Tamil Nadu, the women entrepreneurial development is focused by promoting and encouraging many more Self Help Groups in villages. Some of the achievements of the Self Help Groups are narrated below:

- Many women entrepreneurs are helped by women organisaitons. For example, at Sarthanga Kalingarayan Palayam in Erode District women produce pickle and also run a small super market;
- In Sivathapuram (Salem District) 19 members of a Self Help Group got 2 lakhs loan from Indian Bank and they make anklets and sell them;
- In Erumaipalayam Self Help Women Group bought milch cows and sell milk. So far they have saved 72,000 rupees in Bank;
- In the same village, another group makes plates out of arecanut leaves. This can be used instead of plastic plates. These plates are sent to Five star hotels;
- In Ayothya Patnam, women Self Help Group sells groceries;
- In Perumaanur 20 member women's group owns a tractor and rents it;
- Theni self help women's group went to Ayyampalayam to have a knowledge of candle production.
- In Virudhunagar District, there was a meeting of Self Help Group of women. The collector ordered the officers to look into the 823 appeals of women for starting their own units;
- In Karunkulam, Tuticorin District 7 Self Help Group got a loan of 4.60 lakhs from Pandian Grama Bank to help women entrepreneur;

- Annai Indra Women organization runs the Canteen and Hotel at Madras Secretariat. Women entrepreneurs can sell raw coconut, buttermilk, and they can also conduct tuition for poor students;
- Women entrepreneurs can also run crèches for working women's children;
- In Thalavai Malai Village in Erode District, Miss Poongodi, runs Manonmani Earthworm farm. She has become rich. This can be the natural fertilizer. It is not dangerous to land and foodstuff;
- In Vadipatti, (Madurai district) there is an institutionscalled GRIT, Social organization. It is run by women. They run various organizations like crèche, old age home and family planning centres.

The above programme of Tamil Nadu can be a symbol of the work done in India. Governments may come and go. Leaders may come and go. But men and women have to live. The modern women can try to have the economic and social equality through self help organizations.

Opportunities Available for Women Entrepreneurs in Rural Areas

There are so many opportunities available for women entrepreneurs in the rural areas and the following are some of them:

- Starting of Bio-gas plants
- Planting of mulberry plants
- Introducing Seri-culture in the non-traditional area
- Bee-keeping
- Processing of cereals and pulses
- Basket making
- Dairy farming
- Poultry farming
- Renting of tractors for Agricultural Purpose

- Selling of hot drinks and cool drinks in roadsides
- Aqua culture
- Earthworm fertilizer production etc.

The rural women can make use of the above opportunities. Moreover, women can form a Self Help Group for their development without Government assistance.

Women Entrepreneurship in Reality

Generally women become entrepreneurs after the death of their fathers or husbands. Many Asian women leaders came into politics like that. Today this is not a case. Once women produced pickle, baskets and run typewriting classes etc. But now they run many production and marketing centres of many products. For example Pankajalakshmi has been the director of Padmavathi Corporation for 15 years. Most of the women entrepreneurs are honest. It is note worthy that 99.8 per cent of the women entrepreneurs have repaid the bank loans properly. Women entrepreneurs should not worry about handicap or age. For example Mrs. Lakshmi learnt her job of candle production at the age of 40. Women can achieve in the area of entrepreneurship with the help of enthusiasm and skill.

Present Status of Women Entrepreneurs

Though there is a progress in women entrepreneurship of India, the number of women entrepreneurship is very small. Even today many women live inside the four walls of the house and kitchen. Without utilizing the untapped talents of women, India cannot progress.

For the purpose of encouraging more women to become entrepreneurs, both the Government and the public have to adopt certain strategies in rural areas and that strategies can be the followings:

- Land reforms should be implemented. It should lead to women's ownership of land
- Women should have access to training and technological information
- Loan to SSI may be given to women entrepreneurs at a low interest rate

- Women can run tuition centers in rural areas
- Dry land development programme should be known to rural women
- In all villages apart from agriculture, women should have a part time job, in SSI like match factories
- They can grow vegetable near the houses. The Government can help them by giving them certified seeds etc
- They can make toys and handicrafts and sell them
- They can also produce incense sticks and sell them

The following measures should also be taken up to further improve the status of women:

1. Agrarian reforms should include at least joint ownership of land if not actual ownership of land by women. Such a step would stimulate a chain of changes of relationships, attitudes and perceptions at all levels in the community;
2. At the production level the balance between the cash crops and food crops has to be insisted upon to provide food security to the poor rural women. The long-term impact of food for work programmes vis-à-vis the food aid policies call for a review;
3. Access to training and technological information for agricultural activity has to be provided to women to improve their skills, level of decision-making and effective participation.

Conclusion

In the era of competition, women cannot remain idle inside the house. Women entrepreneur have to play an important role in the development of India and make our nation a developed one. Women's Self Help Groups must be democratic and service minded. These groups should include women of all castes, religions and social status. These women's groups and women entrepreneurs should be creative in future. With hard work and innovative thinking can bring prosperity to the nation and themselves.

Scope and Development of Women Entrepreneurs in Rural Sector

Dr. M. Inbalakshmi

Unemployment is a burning problem for which every citizen should necessarily find a solution. The present economic condition of India does not allow to get sufficient employment. Women are generally ignored whether they are educated or uneducated. Both the educated and uneducated people therefore are in a position to develop their own resource i.e., to seek self employment. We are in the era of globalisation, privatisation and liberalisaiton. Our economy is now kept open, we can also enter freely into other markets, and at the same time on products will be facing competition. Our agriculture sector is now gracing up to meet the challenges posed by globalisation. Our country mainly depends on agriculture for its all round economic development. Nearly 70 per cent of the population depends on agriculture for their livelihood. Government and voluntary organizations are taking sincere steps to generate employment opportunities in the rural sector. By nature rural women are more innovative and more creative with their traditional skills and talents. Hence they are a potential resource in development of entrepreneurship.

It is generally an accepted concept that the male is considered the breadwinner of the family. The female is provided only as a supplementary role to the male dominated society. Due to education and awareness, the concept is slowly changing. The female is slowly emerging as an equal partner to the male in a male dominated society. Infact, an ordinary housewife is discharging the normal functions of management. House management is considered an art, which is discharged only by the female member of the society. She plays the role of a financial adviser, the role of a decision maker, and the right person in time management and so on.

It is an accepted notion that necessity is the mother of invention. Usually woman will become an entrepreneur only in those cases where the head of the family passed away or left the house in distress. Out of compulsion, she will take up the responsibility of running the institution left by her husband. Now the situation is changed. Due to education and because of social compulsion women entrepreneurs coming to the forefront and they are also contributing the share for the development of our economy.

In our country, Non-Government Organizations (NGOs) play a crucial role in the development of women entrepreneurs. They have been providing their services to the rural women not only awareness about sanitation, protected drinking water but also in creating self employment opportunities. While carrying this message to the rural folk, NGOs have been facing a number of problems. We can mention the following:

Factors

1. Lack of support from the members of the family
2. Our social structure is not in favour of encouraging rural women to shoulder the responsibility of running their own units
3. Our rural women have been suffering due to paucity of funds
4. Our beaurcratic structure does not provide helping hands for development of rural women entrepreneurship

5. Lack of education and lack of awareness will be considered another limiting factor.

Government and other voluntary organizations have been addressing the problems mentioned above due to rapid advancement in the communication network. Our rural economy is now integrated with international market. A number of women entrepreneurs have emerged in the sustained efforts of NGOs. Centre for Women Development is created and periodical trainings are provided to the women entrepreneurs.

Role of NGOs

Under the supervision of Tamil Nadu Women Development Centers 'Entrepreneurs Development Programmes' have been successfully running. Till 31.01.2002, 42000 women have undergone Entrepreneurial Development Programmes, the target being 1,18,240. Among the trained a number of women have been earning sufficient income (P. 31 Mutram, Monthly Issue, Jan-Feb 2002.)

Self Help Groups have been organized by the NGOs in the rural areas, in which not less than 10 rural women join together and their savings are circulated among themselves or the savings are deposited with a bank and the bank lends the same to the members to solve their financial problems. Their services include creation of awareness about sanitation, protection of drinking water, wasteland development, rain harvesting and the like.

Their services are also extended to the development of entrepreneurship quality among the rural women folk. They create awareness and self confidence among the rural women to start their own industrial units with a minimal available investment. Banks also help them to solve their financial problems.

Entrepreneurial Activities and Avenues

The selected rural women are highly motivated to start an independent unit. We can mention some other areas in which rural women entrepreneurs have emerged.

1. Now-a-days protection of environment against plastic is an emerging problem for which NGOs try to find a permanent solution by training rural women folk to prepare paper cups, paper bags and paper covers.
2. Efforts are made to preserve and protect our artistic skills in our rural sector. At the same time the skill must be exploited to make it a commercial activity. Our pottery manufacturers are now gearing up to meet the challenges forced by the mechanised sector. Interior decoration is considered one of the components for attracting customers. Our rural folk is now concentrating in the manufacture and marketing of attractive terracotta dolls like horse, elephant, dooms, cages and other decorative items with the help of same raw materials. In Dindigul a woman entrepreneur is successful in manufacturing and marketing terracotta dolls.
3. Self Help Groups in Vallampatti got training in producing PVC pipes and other ancillary materials which are generally used for household wiring and for water connection. After the necessary training they have successfully commissioned their units.
4. The people of New Kokkarapatti village in Dharmapuri District depend only an agriculture even though there is a water problem. They have an opportunity to get help from NGOs and now they are engaged in repairing works like repairing school and other buildings and repairing of drinking water pipes.
5. Training is given to prepare instant food products like murukku mix, Idiappa mix, Ragi flour and wheat flour with less investment. The women entrepreneurs identify the opportunities and make hay.
6. Once a pickle manufacturing was considered an art, now even this art is corporaterised. Women entrepreneurs are now trying in the art of manufacturing of pickles by using preservatives.

7. Due to changes in the food habit people are moving towards tinned food items. With the help of training in the art of preserving dry fish a number of entrepreneurs have taken up this challenging task in the seashore areas and they have proved to be successful in their ventures.
8. Though the law provides that there should not be any discrimination between the male and female labourers, but in practice discrimination does exist. With the help of training provided to women folk, women masons are now slowly competing with male dominated sector. Successful women masons are now turning to be good contractors.
9. Establishment of beauty parlour is a new innovative activity which is going on both in urban centers and in rural centres very successfully. People approach the beauty centers not only for beautification of external appearance but also as a health club to improve the health condition. A number of women entrepreneurs have entered this field after undergoing certain certified courses and they have improved their standard of living, thanks to Mass Media, especially, the Television Channels.
10. Doll making is considered another profitable venture, for women entrepreneurs. In certain colleges training is provided to the women students so that they will have a confidence in carrying out this activity commercially.
11. Due to changes in fashion, the demand for readymade garments is picking up. Even among the women folk demand for readymade blouses is picking up. In Dindigul District, around Natham a Number of Women Entrepreneurs have entered this area also.

Rural Women Entrepreneurs are now playing an important role for the development of rural economy. For the sake of reference a few examples can be cited:

1. Mrs. Vijayalakshmi of Dindigul, the Proprietor of Sriram Apparels in Kavendarpalayam has been successfully running her zurdosi unit after a thirty years struggling and could provide employment to more than 40 unemployed women;
2. Poongodi of Poolampatti has been producing natural fertilizers which is a highly profitable industry just raised from commonly available 'Earthworms';
3. An old student of GTN Arts College by name Mrs. Olive Santhi is a successful entrepreneur in the Fur doll making and painting works. Due to her popularity she has been interviewed in leading Tamil Magazines and she is giving programmes regularly in a famous Tamil Channel regarding doll making. She is an eye-opener for a number of women entrepreneurs. Similarly another girl student from our college has established a beauty parlour in Dindigul and she is a pay-setter for other beauty parlours;
4. India is famous for artistic skills and craftsmanship. Some of the women entrepreneurs have managed to convert waste papers into beautiful toys with the help of the training and motivation provided by 'Tanjore Craft Society'. They are marketing the products not only in Tamil Nadu but also in Kerala, Karnataka and Andhra.

This list goes endless and the contributions of women entrepreneurs have been in the increase. Little drops of water make a mighty ocean. There is no doubt that little contributions from small entrepreneurs lead to our nation's development.

Conclusion

This concept of rural women entrepreneur is only at the infant stage in India. Our social structure has not fully accepted the idea of the women as an equal partner to the male in the society. To overcome this handle education must reach the grass-root level and the society as a whole must provide necessary incentives for the development of women entrepreneurs. It is generally stated that a women is behind every successful man, so the importance of woman cannot neglected. The Government and other voluntary organizations must draw an exhaustive skill for the development of women entrepreneurs. If this is carried out a bright features for the real development of women entrepreneurs is assured.

Women Entrepreneurship—The Need for a Fresh Look

Dr. G. Anjaneya Swamy,
Deepak Raajan

The fact that promotion of entrepreneurship is the key for the economic development of any nation needs no emphasis. As the saying goes "ambition is the index of one's resourcefulness", much of the economic activity therefore depends on the ambitions and aspirations of the people. If India has not economically developed in spite of abundant physical and human resources, the reasons are not far to seek. To use the entrepreneurial jargon, the low level of 'need for achievement' of the people is found to be the primary factor. The conventional assumption that economic development is a function of supply of 'capital' no longer holds good. Now in the fast changing global order, economic development rather is a function of supply of 'people with entrepreneurial abilities.'

An entrepreneur is one who is adept in identifying the business opportunities and exploiting them. In the process, organisations are created to produce want satisfying goods and services. Entrepreneurial activities thus enhance the standard of living of the society. This paper therefore, addresses itself the issues related to women entrepreneurship with a focus on the major constraints faced by rural women. An action plan is extended to help them overcome those constraints. This paper emphasises the need to give women's entrepreneurship a fresh look.

Need for Women Entrepreneurship

Entrepreneurial spirit is not gender specific. Research on entrepreneurship has unequivocally established that entrepreneurial spirit is evenly spread across the population irrespective of caste, creed, gender and religion. It is a different matter if people belonging to some castes and regions have achieved sterling successes than others. The variances in the achievements may largely be due to the variances in the socio-cultural context, political support and economic climate.

As women constitute roughly 50 per cent of the population, it is high time that the fairer sex also is brought into the mainstream economic activity for such an initiative contributes to:

- the optimum utilisation of human resources no matter what the gender is;
- the much talked about women empowerment which in a way depends on economic empowerment;
- help women realise their self-worth by making use their innate potential; and
- channelise the women power towards nation building activities.

It is an irony that in spite of the realisation on the part of the policymakers about the need for promoting women entrepreneurship, the participation of women in the wealth creation process is far from satisfactory. By and large, the pronouncements in this regard have become a political rhetoric. Much needs to be done. Any serious effort to encourage women to participate in entrepreneurial activities in a big way cannot yield the desired results unless the problems or constraints faced by women are properly diagnosed. Therefore the need of the hour is to identify in a systematic way the various bottlenecks and to suggest an action plan leaving the past behind.

Women Entrepreneurship—Common Constraints

Unfavourable Socio-Cultural Milieu

The socio-cultural conditioning that has taken place all through the centuries as to what women should and should not do merit a close examination. The role ascribed to the woman by and large is supportive in nature. It is no surprise that Indian woman is confined to the four walls of the house. She is destined to attend to the domestic chores only. The multifaceted woman's role ranging from being a loyal wife to the husband, a caring mother to the children, a nurturing daughter-in-law to the aged in laws at home—all lay a boundary line within which she operates. Anything that warrants her to go out, not to speak of engaging independently in any serious economic activity outside the home is a taboo. This phenomenon is more pronounced in the rural areas of developing and underdeveloped nations including in India. Nonetheless, occasionally we hear the successes made by women. But the examples are few and far between.

Even in the days of modernisation, it is unfortunate that the chances of mistaking an enterprising woman are more. As such, the societal perceptions of an ideal woman are so different that independent thinking, the desire to be one's own, the ability to translate ideas into action—all get blunted miserably. As a result, the dependence on males has become a rule rather than an exception. The greater such dependence, the closer she is supposed to the ideal woman mould.

The socio-cultural milieu presented thus far, created an unfavourable environment for Indian women to make their mark in entrepreneurial activities. The exact causal factors may vary from place to place. But on the whole, the following attributes are quite discernible:

- Social stigma;
- Male domination;
- Obnoxious family traditions and norms; and
- Absence of property inheritance and consequently economic freedom.

Lack of Role Models

It is a paradox that the land that has given Jhansi Lakshmi Bhai, Sarojini Naidu, Indira Gandhi down to the present Medha Patkar, Kiran Bedi and Kalpana Chawla still has vast masses of women rotting under ignorance, inhibitions, superstition and fear of being branded rebels.

Ironically, Indian mythology and scriptures also played a role in conditioning the women folk into what they are today. Sita, Sati Savitri and Sati Anasuya who toed the line of the husband are classic role models for Indian women. Indian scriptures and religious beliefs made the women to conform their disposition and attributes to the dictates of religions and social norms.

It is a pity that even in the post-independent India, nothing significant has happened to redefine the role of woman. Till recently, the important occupations that an Indian woman could dream of entering are teaching, nursing, personal assistance/secretarial work, etc. Aspiring anything big and different was a matter of social ridicule. It took nearly fifty years for Independent India to see women in unconventional professions/occupations like pilots, police officers, auto and truck drivers, business executives and what not. Still great majority of India women, particularly the rural women are yet to catch up and seize the new opportunities that are coming up in a big way thanks to the spectacular developments taking place in the spheres of science and technology. It is high time that the role of Indian woman is redefined!

Lack of Awareness and Motivation

Lack of awareness and motivation, obviously is the fallout of the factors discussed above. The saying that "even luck does not favour an unprepared mind" is more than true. Entrepreneurial activity in any sphere, centres around human motivation. It triggers the desire to achieve, the urge to excel, the willingness to experiment, the courage to dream and think big and the attitude to question the existing beliefs. The search for opportunities begins. It is the search, inquisitiveness and curiosity which transformed the humans from nomads into settlers, into explorers and conquerors. Much of the progress through the centuries could undoubtedly be attributed to human motivation.

As such, there is an urgent need to instil in the Indian women the confidence that they can achieve. It is heartening to note that in a few pockets of the country the Self Help Groups at the village level like thrift societies, and Mahila Mandals are doing a great job in creating the right awareness among women and channelising their capabilities in more productive ways. The Self Help Groups under DWAKRA scheme in villages of Andhra Pradesh is one of the successful experiments in this regard.

Financial Support

All said and done, however good the idea is, for the conversion of an idea into action, finance is required. At various stages of the implementation/execution of business projects, whether they are large or small, timely availability of financial resource is crucial. As regards finance, women entrepreneurs often are subjected to many hardships. They get a raw deal from many a financial institutions/agencies. It is a vicious circle. The insistence of collateral security for sanctioning the assistance is by and large the biggest stumbling block. Prejudices of the lending agencies in general, absence of property inheritance code, and consequently the inability to offer any 'collateral security' are all linked together.

Misuse of Finance and Incentives

Another strange situation that one comes across is the existence of benami units. To avail the various incentives available to women entrepreneurs. Some unscrupulous men just register the units in the name of the women—be it wife, sister or mother. Such units are women run/managed only on paper. In some cases, the money available in the form of subsidies and even the financial assistance provided by lending agencies by way of loans/advances are squandered by the men who manage. It is viewed as another source of easy money. These unethical practices spell a wrong impression on the concept of women entrepreneurship. As a result, lending agencies are compelled to adopt the famous 'once bitten twice shy' posture when it comes to entertaining the proposals of women entrepreneurs.

The Action Plan

The debate on any issue cannot be fruitful unless it culminates into an action plan. The following initiatives may help in setting the right tone for the promotion of women entrepreneurship:

- *Creation of awareness* about the various business opportunities and the operational aspects in exploiting them. Detailed analysis of the various region specific resources and skills would help in identifying the right opportunities. In a humble way, activities like pickles, incense sticks, ethnic foods, handicrafts, carpets, to name a few, where native wisdom plays an important role, may be encouraged;
- *Spread of information* through mass media, focus group interactive sessions, and extension activities is necessary. Government and NGO's have to take the lead in launching the campaign aimed at enlightening women. Women have to be helped in shedding the age old inhibitions and superstitions. Success stories like Mahila Udyog Vikas (Lijjat pappad) of Maharashtra, the achievements of Self Help Groups in various states have to be forcefully communicated through audio/video presentations in villages;
- Exclusive *entrepreneurial motivation camps* with professional trainers should be organised for the target group of women at the panchayat union level. The participants may be drawn from the villages of the panchayat union. Successful entrepreneurs, social leaders, and acclaimed government servants may be invited to share their experiences which would act as positive reinforcements;

- Introduction of *liberal financial assistance* with easy and flexible terms is another area that needs immediate attention. The approach should be positive. Emphasis needs to be placed on the business potential of the entrepreneurs in paying back the loan amount rather than on collateral security;
- Installation of *stringent punitive measures* to curb the unscrupulous impostors who resort to the misuse of funds. In quite a number of cases, particularly the beneficiaries under various schemes are found to be indulging in lavish lifestyles, wrong application and siphoning off funds to their private accounts. Many lending agencies have their own bitter experiences in this regard. Therefore, appropriate mechanisms need to be installed to monitor the usage of funds.

Conclusion

From the foregoing analysis, it is amply clear that a multi pronged approach needs to be adopted to motivate the women to pursue entrepreneurial activities. The issues involved in the whole exercise are social in nature which calls for a social revolution. Commitment and wholehearted support are crucial for any initiative intended to emancipate Indian women. Concerted effort must be put in to raise the literacy level of the rural women. Education contributes for the awareness and enlightenment. Social activists, NGO's, government agencies and corporate sector should play an active role in the transformation of women, and in driving the rural women to explore entrepreneurial opportunities.

Prospects of Women Entrepreneurs in Rural India

A. Jayarani

Introduction

Women constitute around half of the total world population. So is in India also. Hence, they are regarded as the "better half of the society". The global evidences buttress that women have been performing exceedingly well in different spheres of activities like academics, politics, administration, social work and so on. Now, they have started plunging into industry also and running their enterprises successfully.

Opportunities for Women Entrepreneurs

The Government of India has defined women entrepreneurs based on women participation in equity and employment of a business enterprise.

The Government of India has been assigning increasing importance to the development of women entrepreneurs in the country in recent years. The Sixth Five-years Plan, for example, proposed for promoting female employment in women–owned industries, the government moved a step forward in the Seventh Five-year Plan by including a special scheme on Integration of women in development.

In the recent industrial policy 1991, the Government of India further stressed the need for conducting special entrepreneurs development programmes for women with a view to encourage women to enter industry.

The Government brought out a number of schemes aimed at generating employment. They were Integrated Rural Development Programme (IRDP), Training of Rural Youth for Self-Employment (TRYSEM) and Development of Women and Children in Rural Areas (DWCRA), Supply of Improved Tool-kits to Rural Artisans (SITRA), Jawahar Rozgar Yojana (JRY), Swarnajayanti Gram Swarozgar Yojana (SGSY) and so on. These programmes in general were aimed at providing supplementary employment opportunities, imparting skills needed for self-employment and employment through social asset creation.

In order to provide opportunity for women entrepreneurs, formation of Self Help Groups (SHGs) for rural (unemployed) women entrepreneurs. The SHGs not only provide the members with an opportunity to carry out economic activities, but also discuss and analyze their social and economic situations to arrive at the root cause of their problems and strive to find and implement solutions.

Commercial banks, in collaboration with District Rural Development Agency, played a key role in advancing loans to the women groups in improving their economic status. Further, income generation is an integral part of Self Help Groups under DWCRA scheme and training provides an opportunity to learn from their own family members.

A women entrepreneur can start an enterprise at a small scale. There are a number of women entrepreneurs who have started small enterprises but later expanded them to large scale units.

SIDBI and NABARD must continue to support the SHGs/NGOs/Banks in imparting training to women members and assist them by providing liberal credit.

Conclusion

A large number of employment can be generated only through making many people entrepreneurs who would in turn generate employment opportunities not only for themselves but also for others.

Even though there are many hurdles involved in the process of promoting micro-enterprises through SHGs, the attempt is worthwhile one and the sustained efforts by the government, NGOs, and SHGs in the long-run can generate huge employment opportunities among the rural women entrepreneurs and thus eradicate poverty among the rural masses.

Rural Women Entrepreneurs Constraints

Dr. S. Murugesan

Introduction

In traditional societies women had been confined to the four walls of home, children, household affairs and family rituals and costumes. Very few had the opportunity to come out of the four walls and shine in different spheres.

In recent years women have come in forefront in different walks of life and are competing successfully with men. This has been possible because of education. Political awakening, legal safeguards, urbanization and social reforms.

Social Constraints

The constraints which women entrepreneurs are facing in starting a new venture arranging the initial finance, marketing the products and complying with various rules and regulations.

In many developing countries, marriage is the only career for most women. Professionally women have confined their activities to such areas as education, office work, nursing, medicine, engineering, information technology and fashion technology. It is only rarely that they enter trade, business. Women have been victims of social prejudices and assumptions, women are weak, passive, people oriented and dependent.

Limited exposure and failure to understand and take risk further inhibit them. The net result is limited achievement. The negative self image comes in their way to take up new jobs, new responsibilities and risks which are must for women entrepreneurs.

Financial Constraints

The need for fixed and working capital should be adequately met if the new enterprises are to survive and grow. The lake of financial resources deter potential young entrepreneurs to start new ventures. The insistence by the commercial banks for security against loans creates complications for those who do not own land/building or their property which may be acceptable to the bank.

Overcome the Barriers

The Government of Tamil Nadu assists women entrepreneurs through different agencies such as Small Industries Development Corporation (SIDCO), District Industrial Center (DIC), Tamil Nadu Industrial Center (TIC) and Small Scale Industries (SSI) in preparing project reports meeting the cost of machinery, building and training, hiring of managerial personnel. In certain cases 100 per cent cost of technical expert is met by the state for a period of one year. Industrial enterprises started by women enjoy six years exemption from the payment of sales taxes.

In international and traditional trade fairs, the products manufactured by women entrepreneurs should be widely displayed. The Government of India should provide necessary literature, course books and publications for the benefit of women.

Conclusion

In business field the entry of a woman is a relatively new phenomena. The enterprises set up by them are mostly in small-scale sector. On their own part, to perform well women have to overcome their own limitations. They must reach out for new plan, new responsibilities and new entrepreneur.

Self Help Groups and Entrepreneurial Development in Rural Areas

Dr. C. Azhakappan

Economic development plays an important role in the development and growth of any society. The importance of promoting women to engage in economic activities is being increasingly realized in all developing countries. The need is two fold:

(i) to empower women by bringing them into the main stream of development and improving their economic status; and

(ii) to provide new employment opportunities by way of income generation, self employment and entrepreneurship to women from different socio-economic sectors.

The New Industrial Policy has the strategy for the hostile development of women. This would help to develop their personality and at the same time improve their economic and social conditions. This policy, with the end in view, has re-defined "Women's Units" as units in which they had a majority share holding and management control. In this context, an attempt is made to assess the entrepreneurial role of women units, namely, Self Help Groups in the alleviation of rural poverty.

In India, since 1994, United Nations Development project has been under the implementation. For this the districts are characterised by high level of social stratification with high levels of poverty, caste differentiation, severe ecological degradation, landlessness and landlordism, poor transport infrastructure, high prevalence of child labour, child marriage, high under employment due to droughts, low wages, high infant mortality and recurring epidemics like measles. According to participatory poverty assessments, households with female heads, single parents and elderly with no support mechanisms are extremely poor.

The main focus of activity of the SHGs is to generate savings for income-generating projects in the village. The seed capital is provided by UNDP. This has pioneered a unique participatory method for the identification of ventures as well as beneficiaries at the grossroots level in the spirit of planning from below. Although the entry point of the project is mainly credits and savings, the SHGs benefit the people in every aspect of life in a village community.

Enabling women to help themselves through entrepreneurship, it raises their sense of self-worth, making them even more eager to be productive members of society. These benefits indicate the worthiness and viability of assisting entrepreneurial women in the developing world, though multiple challenges still exist. Greater and continue support for entrepreneurial activities is needed to further improve the lives of these women and the condition of their communities.

Sustainability of Self Help Groups—An Analysis

Dr. S. Krishnamurthy

Introduction

The agriculture, though remains main activity in rural areas, most of the rural people could not depend on it solely for their livelihood. As the monsoon plays havoc often, the income from agriculture almost becomes irregular. Hence the poverty becomes the order of the day in the rural areas and especially among the women in general. It is so because, of the 51.98 million females engaged in agriculture and allied activities, 45 per cent were employed as agricultural labourers compared to which only 21 per cent of male workers as agricultural labourers. Moreover womens' access to land ownership is extremely limited. If at all, they get any work, they are employed only for 90 to 100 days in a year. Hence they lead very miserable life in comparison to other sections of the people of our country.

Self Help Groups (SHGs)—New lease of Life of Rural Masses

Now-a-days SHGs are gaining popularity in rural areas. The SHGs are considered a new lease of life for the women in villages for their social and economic empowerment.

As the SHGs are recent phenomena, the question will arise about their sustainability in future. Though success of SHGs depend on many factors like government patronages, the efficiency of NGOs etc., the positive attitude of SHGs members towards their SHGs assume paramount importance. As the membership of SHGs is a voluntary one, the sustainability of the SHGs depend on sincere and regular participation of their members. At the same time the members will be sincere to their SHGs only when they feel that the SHGs are serving the causes of the members better.

Hence an attempt has been made in this study to assess the attitude of SHGs members towards their SHGs by selecting 75 members randomly from SHGs formed at Bodinayakanur block in Theni district.

Measurement of Attitude of SHGs Members

Attitudes are evaluative statements or judgments concerning objects, people or events. Hence, the attitude may be positive or negative.

The Attitude scale has been used in this study to measure the overall attitudes of the sample respondents. The following relevant statements have been presented to respondents to assess their attitudes towards their SHGs:

Statements of Evaluation

The formation of SHGs resulted in:

1. Equal status for women in household;
2. Equal status for women in community and village level;
3. Equal access over resources at household level;
4. Breaking social and cultural barriers to the development of women;
5. Providing political empowerment to the women members;
6. Greater access to women for financial resources;
7. Increase in the income level of women;
8. Financial self-reliance of women;
9. Awareness of health, education etc;
10. Better communication skills;

11. Better leadership skills;
12. Improved functional literacy;

The respondent is asked to agree or disagree with these statements. Then each response is given numerical score as given below so as reflect its degree of attitude favourableness.

Strongly agree	-	5
Agree	-	4
No opinion	-	3
Disagree	-	2
Strongly Disagree	-	1

The response value of each statement should be added to know the total score of the each respondent, which will be in between 12 and 60.

SHG Members and Their Level of Attitudes

The sample SHG members are classified into two categories as average and above and below average categories on the basis of their attitude level scores. The respondents are classified as above on the basis of Arithmetic mean value. The Arithmetic mean value of 75 respondents covered under this study is 53.39. The respondents to have scored 53.39 and above are considered to have average and above average level of attitude. While those who have scored below 53.39 were considered to have below average level of attitude.

The level of attitudes of respondents are classified above are presented in the table given below.

Level of Attitudes of Respondents

Level	No. of Respondents	Percentage to Total
Average and above	43	57
Below average	32	43
Total	**75**	**100**

It could be inferred from the above table that majority of SHG members are having positive attitude towards their

SHGs. It is found that 57 per cent of the members are fully satisfied with operational performances of the SHGs. Here, it could be safely assumed that these members will continue their membership in their respective SHGs.

The above table also indicates that around 43 per cent of the members are not fully satisfied with SHGs. If these members begin to show disinterest in the activities of the SHGs, the sustainability of those SHGs will become doubtful one. There SHGs initially may become sick and finally they may be closed.

Conclusion

It is duty of the promoting agency i.e. NGOs and the government to assess the attitude of SHG members in regular basis. The success of any SHG depends on the active participation of all members. If some of the members are dissatisfied, group cohesiveness will be affected which in turn, will weaken the performance of SHGs. Hence the promoting agency must monitor continuously over all attitude of SHG members pertaining to their respective SHGs. These measures will help to identify the members who remain dissatisfied. Now necessary corrective actions may be taken to remove the causes for such dissatisfaction. These measures will certainly strengthen all SHGs.

References

1. Lalitha, N. *Self Help Groups in Rural Development,* Dominant Purchasers and Distributors, New Delhi, 2002.
2. Pillai, J.K. *Women and Empowerment,* Gyan Publishing House, New Delhi, 1995.
3. Manivannan, R. *Innovations in Rural Lending: Self Help Groups,* Indian Overseas Bank Monthly News Review, 5 (6), June 2nd 1992.
4. The Hindu Date 15th June, 1992.
5. The Business Line 23rd December, 2002.

Role of Entrepreneurship Development Programme for Women in Tamil Nadu—A Study with Reference to Tanwa Unit of Dombuchery

S. Balamurugan

Introduction

Women in India still perform only their traditional roles in their houses and in agriculture. They do not engage in any of the economic activities without assistances from their men-folk. Due to socio-cultural, traditional practices and conventions and taboos, the development of women entrepreneurship is very low in our country. This is absolutely true in the case of rural women, though the urban women are slightly enjoying better status in the society. Though women represents 50 per cent of the total population, there are only 2,95,680 women entrepreneurs of the total 2.64 million entrepreneurs in India during the year 1998-99. It shows that they do not have any economic independence in the society as well as their poor contribution to the economy of our country.

Rationale for Development of Women Entrepreneurs

The noble scholar and Indian economist Mr. Amarthya Sen expressed in his words, "Unless Women are empowered, issues like literacy, health, population explosion will remain unresolved problems of developing countries". Hence the development of women entrepreneurship is very much essential not only for the economic empowerment but also for well being of the whole country. Moreover there are many case studies which found that women possess a futuristic outlook and the capacity to nurture new enterprises. But in India, women could not shine in their life because of male reservations towards them. This attitude of reservation creates many problems for women at various levels like family support, training, licensing, banking and marketing.

Entrepreneurship Development Programme (EDP) for Women in Tamil Nadu

Tamil Nadu Government has announced in assembly on 25.05.2001, a scheme for training five lakhs women in entrepreneurial skill for self-employment. The Government wants to achieve the above target before 2006. Accordingly it likes to cover nearly 1 lakh women each year under EDP.

The scheme covers the women of the following categories:

1. To give additional training to those women who possess some skill on particular business;
2. To give practical training to those women who possess only theoretical knowledge;
3. To give training on particular skill development to those women who possess neither theoretical or practical knowledge.

Workings of EDP Conducted by Government of Tamil Nadu

Tamil Nadu Government has appointed Tamil Nadu Corporation for Women Development (TCWD) as a nodal agency to undertake training programmes for prospective women entrepreneurs in Tamil Nadu. The TCWD is implementing this scheme with other Government agencies like Directorate of Industry and Commerce, Tamil Nadu Backward Commission, District Industrial Centers etc.

This EDP has been designed by the Government to achieve the following objectives:

1. To give economic and social empowerment to the women;
2. To create conducive atmosphere for women to take up various entrepreneurial activities;
3. To increase the overall income of the women;
4. To bring out the various talents possessed by the women in general.

In keeping with the above objectives, the TCWD through its co-ordinating agencies, conducts training programmes on various skill development. After completion of the training programme, it assists the women trainees to form Self Help Groups (SHG) or any other women organisations like Tamil Nadu Women in Agriculture (TANWA) etc. to take up a particular venture collectively. Moreover this corporation takes necessary steps to provide adequate finance by the commercial banks. Likewise it assists the individual prospective women entrepreneur to avail credit facilities directly from the bank.

Evaluation of Entrepreneurial Development Programme

An attempt has been made to study the impact of Entrepreneur Development Programme Conducted by TCWD in socio-economic empowerment of women trainees. The TANWA unit was started in Dombuchery on 21-10-2002. This unit is having 20 women members. Though TANWA is meant for imparting training to women on skill development in agricultural operations, the same women members are also given various skill training under EDP. This unit member has undergone training on various agricultural operations for 5 days starting from 21-10-2002. The same members were also given training under EDP for 7 days starting from 16-12-2002. The opinions about impact of EDP on the women trainees are collected with the help of questionnaire schedule and the consolidated results have been presented in the table given below.

From the following table, it could be observed that, the training progammes have positive impact on the trainees.

Economic and Social Impact of EDP on TANWA Women members-Dombuchery

Sl. No.	Nature of Impact	Percentage To Total
1.	Increase in Self Confidence	70
2.	Increase in Family Welfare Awareness	76
3.	Increase in status in the society	75
4.	Increase in knowledge on related skill	85
5.	Increase in regular earnings of family	75
6.	Help in repayment of loan	80
7.	Avoiding Money lenders	65

Source: Primary Data.

All the women respondents opined that they have achieved both social and economic status in the society after having become earning members. They could become earning members only after having attended the training conducted under EDP. Nearly 70 per cent of the respondents felt that they are now more self-reliant in their day-to-day activities. Another important findings of the study are that earnings by these women entrepreneurs really are augmenting the financial resources of the particular family. These additional earnings by these women give the position of equal status with their male counterparts. Moreover it was also found that by forming a group, these new women entrepreneurs begin to wield considerable influence in respect of local matters.

Now they also feel that there is a ready market for most of the products in the local areas itself, which were not fully served earlier. The women who attended the training immediately started manufacturing washing powder, phenol and other household items. They have started earning the profit out of their ventures. But at the same time, they could not undertake these ventures on large scale due to the financial constraints. Though the banks are providing some financial assistance, the members feel that the assistance is not forthcoming in adequate amount and in right time.

Hence the Government should see that financial assistances should not be stumbling block for these prospective women entrepreneurs. The Government should also ensure that loan applications are quickly processed with minimal procedures by lending banks. The prospective women entrepreneurs also face problems in expanding the size of the markets. Though they are successful in local markets, they could not expand their market to district or state levels. Here the women entrepreneurs expect the assistances from the Government. In this regard the Government can help them by conducting exhibitions at the district centers where the products produced by the women entrepreneurs may be exhibited. This will increase the size of market which in turn, increases the overall profit of the women entrepreneurs.

Another important grievance of the women are that after having become entrepreneur they are to manage the all household works by themselves without getting any assistances from their male counterparts. Hence the women generally feel that they are over burdened now. Such extra pressure affects their efficiency while performing their duties. Hence they expect their male counterparts to perform some of the household works. Hence the role of men are equally important in making the women successful in their carriers.

Women Entrepreneurs in Rural India

Dr. V.M. Selvaraj

Introduction

The progress of a country involves not merely economic but also social and institutional changes. In many underdeveloped countries, it calls for a new set of values and new concepts of society and Government. India is a country of villages and so the development of the country mainly depends upon the all-round progress of the rural areas. Mahathma Gandhi, the Father of the Nation wrote long back in 1936 in Harijan, "I have believed and repeated times without number that India is to be found not in its few cities but in its 7,00,000 villages.... I would say that if the villages perish, India with perish too". Rural development is advocated today as a basic strategy for all-round development of countries like India. In this context, the importance of rural development is fully realised. Without proper rural development, there cannot be any economic growth or social upliftment. For this, rural industrialisation is must. In this article, women entrepreneurs in rural areas are discussed.

Women constitute 46.5 per cent of total population. 28.9 per cent of work force and 11 per cent of entrepreneurs.

Entrepreneurship development depends not only on economic factors but also on socio-cultural indices.

Entrepreneurship

The term 'entrepreneur' refers to an individual who provides the fourth factor of production namely enterprise. According to Noah Webster, "Entrepreneur is one who assumes the risk and management of business".

Entrepreneurship is a process involving various actions to be undertaken to establish an enterprise. In short, it is a process of giving birth to a new enterprise.

According to Schampeter "Entrepreneurship is based on purposeful and systematic innovation. It included not only the independent businessman but also company directors and managers who actually carry out innovative functions". Entrepreneurship precedes industrialisation. Rural entrepreneurship can be defined as entrepreneurship emerging in rural areas in rural entrepreneurship. Rural entrepreneurship refers to the process of establishing industrial units in the rural areas. That is, rural entrepreneurship implies rural industrialisation.

Indian women are patient in nature and do have the capacity to accept things. The development of women entrepreneur would be the appropriate approach to fight against poverty at the grassroot and generate income at the household level.

In the modern era, women education is given importance at all levels. The percentage of women's participation in working group is increasing. In India, 94 per cent of the women are engaged in the unorganised sector of the economy, 81.4 per cent in agriculture and the rest in non agricultural occupations (Govt. of India, 1974).

The present study aims to analyse the various opportunities which are available to rural women entrepreneurs.

Institutional Support

In India, women are engaged in manufacturing and trading for a long time. Nearly 80 per cent of Indian women are in rural areas and 90 per cent of rural and 70 per cent of urban working women are unskilled creating and developing their skills through skill training and entrepreneurship. Therefore, some support should be given to improve their performance. Government of India and Tamil Nadu provides some support to the rural women entrepreneurs to improve their performance.

Banks play a key role in promoting women entrepreneurship through various Government programmes. As per the recommendations of National perspective plan for women, Women Development Corporations have been set up. At present such corporations are functioning in 17 states and these corporations provide various support to the rural women entrepreneurs. The Government of India has introduced several other women oriented schemes. Among the schemes some of the schemes are given below:

1. Support to Training and Employment Programmes (STEP) for women;
2. Development of women and Children in Rural Areas (DWCRA);
3. Mahila Samriddhi Yojana (MSY);
4. Rashtriya Mahila Kosh (RMK).

NABARD has been making efforts to establish linkages between Self Help Group organised by some voluntary agencies for poor people in rural areas and official credit for production purposes and reduce their dependence on informal credit sources.

NABARD prepared guidelines for promoting group activities under DWCRA programme and provided 100 per cent refinance support.

NABARD started playing attention to "gender" issues in credit and support services since July 1992 by setting up of a women's cell in its Head office at Mumbai. It introduced the following women oriented schemes:

1. Assistance to Rural Women in Non-farm Development (ARWIND);

2. Women Development Cell; and
3. Linking Self Help Groups (SHGs) with banks.

Swarna Jayanti Gram Swarozgar Yojana, involving the Self Help Group concept, has been launched to provide self employment and economic empowerment to the rural poor on the initiation of the Ministry of Rural Development. It has been decided in a national conference in June 2001, to raise the members of Self Help Groups in the country, from the existing 5.11 lakhs to 10 lakhs by the year 2004, so as to have at least one viable Self Help Group in each rural habitation in the country.

Self Help Groups play a vital role in rural development in general and for rural women in particular Self Help Group is formed on the following two major principles.

(i) Rural women are poor and capable of saving;

(ii) Rural women are poor and good credit risk.

A Self Help Group may consist of 10-20 persons belonging to families below the poverty line and a person should not be a member of more than one group. In case of minor irrigation scheme or in the case of disabled person, this number may be a minimum of five. The concept of SHG, (Self Help Group) moulds women as a responsible citizen of the country achieving social and economic status. Women led SHGs in many parts of the country have achieved success in brining the women to the mainstream of decision making. The SHGs in our country has become a source of inspiration for women welfare. It is also a viable organised setup to disburse micro credit to the rural women and encouraging them to enter into entrepreneurial activities.

Rural women within the same village can form a Self Help Group for the following objectives:

(i) To enable members to become self dependent and self reliant;

(ii) To form a forum for members to discuss their social and economic problems;

(iii) To develop the decision making capacity of members;

(iv) To promote thrift and cooperation among the members;

(v) To provide organisational strength to the members.

The SHG can obtain loan from commercial banks. The banks provide loans to SHGs on the basis of their business transactions. For the first six months how much the SHG has transacted may be issued as the loan amount. If the first loan is repaid then two times more than the first loan may issued as a second loan. The members of the SHG decide the rate of interest to be charged from its members when loan is sanctioned to its members. The members may avail the benefit of loan. The members may increase their business activities. The performance of SHG is good.

A simple practical situation is given. The activities of a SHG for the month of December 2002 given below:

Nature of work	Monthly production	Expenditure	Profit
Washing powder	100 kgs	Rs. 2,200	Rs. 700
Cleaning powder	50 kgs	Rs. 300	Rs. 75
Sottu Neelam	6 litres	Rs. 150	Rs. 45
Masala power	30 kgs	Rs. 1,000	Rs. 200
Total		**Rs. 3,650**	**Rs. 1,020**

$$\text{Rate of profit on cost} = \frac{1020}{3650} \times 100 = 25\%$$

This data is collected from a SHG, which functions in a village situated in Sankarankovil taluk.

The SHG of the village earns a profit of 25 per cent on total cost. But they find it very difficult to market their products. Formation of SHG helps in the eradication of unemployment problems.

Various types of loans are issued to women entrepreneurs under the following scheme:

1. SGSY
2. KVIC
3. PMRY
4. SHG.

No subsidy is given under SHG scheme.

Areas

Following are the areas which are suitable to Indian Women Entrepreneurs. The areas may differ from place to place.

1. Coir products
2. Coconut shell products
3. Ceramic units
4. Cattle feeds
5. Telecommunications, Fax, Operation services
6. Lime powder
7. Toy making with different types of raw materials
8. Dairy units
9. Sericulture
10. Handloom weaving units, Pickles, Jams and Jellies making
11. Poultry units
12. Cotton Textiles
13. Bricks making
14. Wood and Wooden products
15. Bakery

Many number of areas are available to rural women entrepreneurs. But among them only a few areas are stated above.

Findings and Suggestions

A large number of opportunities are available to rural women entrepreneurs. But, they face many difficulties:

(i) They find very difficult to market their products. Their products are to be advertised. But it may involve some more expenses. Due to this, their profit or income may be reduced;

(ii) The lower and middle class women entrepreneurs feel inferiority complex;

(iii) Lack of confidence in their own abilities;

(iv) Financial constraints;

(v) Problem of procuring sufficient raw materials;

(vi) Indian women entrepreneurs are handicapped by lack of technical knowhow;

(vii) Banks and other financial institutions have negative attitude towards women entrepreneurs;

(viii) Normally, rural women are forced to involve in household activities and agricultural activities.

In order to remove the above difficulties, the following steps may be taken.

(i) To sell the products, co-operative advertisement may be given;

(ii) Women entrepreneurship awareness must be created among the rural women entrepreneurship;

(iii) Financial support must be given to rural women entrepreneur. Women entrepreneurs may also try to utilise the following schemes to mobilise funds.

(a) Group Loan.

(b) S.G.S.Y.

(c) TAHDCO.

(iv) The Government should take full responsibility for providing raw material.

If the above steps are followed then rural women may participate in the process of economic development of India.

REFERENCES

1. Radha Raman Singh and Rabindra Narayanan Singh, *"IRDP and Revitalisation of Rural Scene in India"*, Khadigramodyog. January, 1985.
2. Dwarakanath, *"Rural Credit and Women Self Help Groups"*, Kurukshetra, November, 2002.
3. Prasant Sarangi, *"Self Help Groups—An Experiment in Orissa"*. Kurukshetra, Feb., 2003.
4. Soundarapandian, M., *"Women Entrepreneurship—Issues and Strategies"*.

Challenges of Rural Women Entrepreneurs

Miss. S. Jeyarani
Dr. M. Dhanabalan

Introduction

The position of women in India has always been a rather ambivalent one in our culture. On the one side, she has resin to the status of divinity and on the other side, she is being exploited as somebody lower in status to men in every life style. However, towards the end of the nineteenth century, it would be true to say that the women have started coming out of their home for education. Moreover, women have come in the forefront in different walks of life and are competing successfully with men despite the social, psychological and economical barriers.

The recent years, an increasing tendency among women to take up employment to supplement their family income has been found throughout the nation. The economic compulsion coupled with high cost of living together has urged for better standard additional luxuries has led more women to take up employment.

Socio-economic advancement of a country can be judge best by the status and position, which it can bestow on its women. The female population constitutes nearly half of the total population. According to the 1991 census, the total population of India was 843.9 million, of which women population amounted to 406.3 million. The size of women population in India indicates the potential strength of women in the total human resource in the country.

According to 1991 census, self-employed women constitute 12.3 per cent of the total number against 5.2 per cent in 1981 census. But the women representation in gainful employment is comparatively low. There is a wide gap between potential and utilisation of women in our country.

Maharashtra is advanced in industries and are leading in textiles. It has ranked first in industrial production, followed by West Bengal, Gujarat and Tamil Nadu. There are bright prospects for women entrepreneurs through many schemes such as Rural Development Programme, Indira Mahila Yojana (IMY), Rashtriya Mahila Kosh (RMK), STEP, NORAD Programme, ARVIND started by NABARD, DWCRA and TRYSEM. But the problem is that the rural women are no aware and literate on hour to handle all the legal and other formalities involving in loan availing and establishing in industrial unit. They also lack confidence in their ability to run the entrepreneurship. Though women constitute almost half of the world population, their representation in gainful employment is comparatively low. However in recent years, women have come in the forefront in different lifestyles.

There are several factors, which induce women to become entrepreneurs. The factors can be broadly classified under two, namely pull factors and push factors. Under the first category, women entrepreneurs choose the profession as a challenge, with an urge to do something new, personal liking for a business or to have an independent occupation. The other category of women take up business enterprise to get over financial difficulties and responsibilities thrust on them due to family circumstances.

Problems of Rural Women Entrepreneurs

The problem or difficulty of a women entrepreneur is that she is a woman. Therefore, the attitudes of society towards her and the constraint in which she has to live and work creates difficulties and problems at all levels, i.e., family support, training, banking, licensing and marketing. Women still suffer from male reservation about their role and capacity.

The rural women entrepreneurs are confronting with several problems particularly in the areas of production, marketing, finance, management, technology, social and psychological and employment. It has known that the rural woman entrepreneur has shortage of working capital due to inadequate sanctioning of loans by the commercial banks. The returns for the investment are not sufficient to meet the cost of borrowing and hence some of the units, not found economically viable in operation.

Proper awareness does not exist among the rural women entrepreneurs as to the various issues relating to the legal formalities of operating enterprise in India. Majority of the rural women entrepreneurs have lack of knowledge about agencies and institution working entrepreneurs, various schemes run by government, raw material availability, availability of machinery and equipment, marketing, different laws/legal aspects, merits and demerits of various enterprises, various improved technologies and loaning schemes and procedures of financial institutions. Social attitudes prevent proper training for rural women, who can therefore act only as helpers. They cannot act independently.

The various problems faced by the rural women entrepreneurs can be classified into five categories and are as follows:

1. *Industrial Problems*

The beauticians faces problems in industries like, lack of continual supply of raw-materials for an interrupted production, lack of sufficient stock of raw-material in period of short supply and anticipated change in price time consuming procedure of procurement of raw-material, variations in the prices of raw-materials at different places, lack of marketing experience, competition from established and larger units in the production line, delayed disposal of produce, difficulty in getting money from buyer after sale and lack of sufficient finished goods for smooth sale operation and lack of efficient customer service.

The hurdles are not over as the vicious one comes now. And that is marketing—both of raw material and of finished goods. To market her product she has to be at the mercy of middlemen who eat up a big chunk of profit. Here the middlemen try to exploit rural women entrepreneurs at both ends. They deny her discount or give the minimum discount in the purchase of raw material and on the other hand try to extract maximum credit discount and commission on purchase of finished products from her.

If she decides to eliminate middlemen, it involves lot of running around. Secondly, in these days of stiff competition huge sum of money is required for advertisement. If the product happens to be a consumer commodity, then it takes time to win people away from other products and make this product popular. And then the tendency is to always question the quality of the product produced by rural women entrepreneurs, though many agree that rural women entrepreneurs are more sincere in maintaining the quality and time schedule.

2. ***Financial Problems***

Limited working capital, constant need of finance, inadequate amount advanced through financing agencies, difficulty in justifying claim for finances, economic incredibility of women and lack of collateral security do the rural women entrepreneurs face the various financial problems.

But the biggest catch is that of collateral security which is required to get bank credit. And rural women generally do not have any property in their names. House or property is mostly in the names of fathers, brothers or husbands. Rural women may have some jewels but even that they cannot give as security without consent of the husbands or male members of family. And family members do not like to risk their capital in ventures started by rural women. Basically, there is a lack of confidence in a rual women's ability. They may risk all family fortune for their sons or male member's business. For this they even persuade women to part with their jewels but are not ready to invest anything in the projects of rural women members.

Procedures of bank loans and delay in the running about involved deter many rural women from venturing. At the government level, the licensing authorities and labour officers and sales tax inspector throw up humiliating questions like what technical qualifications have they, how will manage labourers? How will they manage both house and business? Does their husband approve? etc.

3. *Management and Technical Problems*

The rural women entrepreneurs face the problem of inadequate incentives provided by the Governments, long and complicated procedures to avail institutional help, many formalities and paper work delay sanction, non-co-operative attitude of the employees, frequent visits to institution, personal or political influences needed to avail institutional help quickly, bribery in the agencies providing subsidies/incentives/loans, target oriented approaches and lack of promotional and effective communication between field functionaries and rural women entrepreneurs, lack of communication and co-ordination between different agencies, lack of media support to update the knowledge and skill, of opportunities to acquire business skill, harassment of officials in completion of documents and other formalities, lack of infrastructure facilities, insufficient of skilled workers and experienced workers leave the unit after sufficient exposure.

4. *Social and Psychological Problems*

The various social and psychological problems faced by the rural women entrepreneurs are lack of self-motivation, lack of motivation from family and society, conflicts due to dual responsibilities, non-co-operative attitude of husband and family members, no appreciation for independent decision, non-consistent of traditional norms, lack of recognition and appreciation, in the family, male dominance, lack of social contacts and lack of confidence in women's ability.

In rural areas joint families are still the norm. The overbearing presence of elders restrain even young men from venturing out; so one can imagine how much a young girl needs to put up to become economically independent. They are costly engaged in low paid, backbreaking agricultural activities or act as helpers in handicrafts. It is not that rural women do not have skills or capacity but they are nor property trained or inculcated in craftsmanship because it is felt that if a skill is imparted to a girl it is wasted because when she gets married she takes away the skill with her.

5. *General Problems*

The general problems are excessive burden of work and responsibility, health problems, lack of leisure time and other activities, excessive tensions and challenges, less change prone, lacks systematic planning and working, incompetent in handling technical, financial, sale production and other managerial activities, poor risk taking ability, inadequate credit orientation, lack of emotional maturity.

Majority of the rural women entrepreneurs have lack of knowledge about agencies and institution working entrepreneurs, various schemes run by Government, raw-material availability, availability of machinery and equipments, marketing, different laws/legal aspects, merits and demerits of various enterprises, various improved technologies and loaning schemes and procedures of Financial Institution.

Suggestions

Government should improve publicity regarding the incentives/concessions and organise more awareness programme to rural women entrepreneurs through various media.

The rural women entrepreneurs should make use of the various incentive schemes offered by the Government.

Government should encourage private training institution involved in rural women entrepreneurs' development by offering incentives.

Persuade women to form themselves into Self Help Groups and make use of micro-credit efficiently.

Conclusion

It has felt that proper publicity campaign to be set up/ organised facilities, incentives and programmes available for rural women entrepreneurs in India. It is equally imperative that the Government and the financial institutions including assistance to rural women entrepreneurs as well as the existing enterprises operated by the rural women entrepreneurs.

References

1. Medha Dubhashi Vinze, *Women Entrepreneurship in India,* Mittal Publication, Delhi, 1987.
2. Kamal Singh, *Women Entrepreneurs, Asia Publishing House,* New Delhi, 1992.
3. Dr. A.K. Chaudhary, *Rural Women Entrepreneurship in India: Bright Prospects,* Kurushetra, June 1998.
4. P. Saravanavel, *Entrepreneurial Development, Principles, Policies and Programmes,* Ess Pee Kay Publishing House, Madras, 1997.

Financial and Social Constraints of Rural Women Entrepreneur in Thanjavur District

S. Kamaraju

An entrepreneur is one who changes the resources of production into products and thereby influencing the rate of economic growth of a nation. A woman is self-employed if she runs a small business enterprise and looks after business alone. If the business venture is started by a woman in a small scale and a few people are employed to keep it running, the woman herself act as manager, then the woman is an entrepreneur. A woman entrepreneur could be defined as an adult woman who undertakes to organize, own and run an enterprise.

The erstwhile Thanjavur district was trifurcated into three districts namely Thanjavur, Nagapattinam and Thiruvarur. The important areas come under Thanjavur districts are Thanjavur, Thiruvaiyaru, Papanasam, Kumbakonam, Orathanad, Pattukkottai and Peravuruni. It is bounded by Perambalur district in the north, Palkstraight and Pudukkottai in the south, Tiruchirapalli and Pudukkottai in the west and Thiruvarur distirct in the east.

Thanjavur is an agricultural district which has been carrying out agricultural operations for a long time. Agriculture is the main source of income. But there has been a changing scenario till the recent past. Agricultural income started dwindling due to poor or failure of monsoon and late release of water or lack of water in Cauvery. This situation compelled the people to find an alternative and to seek income from other sources. Women in this district are not an exception and they also engage themselves in small scale business and investment activities due to necessity.

Keeping this in mind the present study, "Financial and Social Constraints of Rural Women Entrepreneurs in Thanjavur district", made an attempt to study about the women entrepreneurs in Thanjavur district.

The list of women entrepreneurs was collected from the office of the Village Panchayat Board Presidents while selecting the women entrepreneurs engaged in illegal business (illicit brewing) and who gave up the business, and the units run by men in the names of women entrepreneur were eliminated from the list. A sample of 120 women entrepreneurs were identified in five taluks namely Papanasam, Thiruvaiyaru, Orathanad, Pattukkottai and Thanjavur. They are engaged in various kinds of entrepreneurial activities like milk farming, tailoring units, food products, petty shop, grocery shop, flour mill and wet grinding, typewriting institute, mate making, soft drinks, rice mill, fertilizer shop, jaggary, confectionery units, bread manufacturing, catering, oil seeds processing and cattle rearing.

Among the 120 women entrepreneurs, only 30 entrepreneurs are having a sizeable business. The information pertaining to type of trade, number of entrepreneurs, total amount of investment and number of employees are furnished hereunder *(See Table 24.1).*

The study reveals that the number of women entrepreneurs having sizeable business in milk farming is 10. Milk farming is popular in Thanjavur district because of the availability of the traditional knowledge regarding the management of the milk farming and the availability of fodder for milch animals. In addition to this, artificial insemination centres are functioning at important centres and a big milk

Table 24.1. Trade, Investment and Persons Employed by Entrepreneurs

Trade	Number of Entrepreneurs	Investments (Rs.)	Number of employees
Milk farming	10	2,50,000	50
Petty shop	5	25,000	10
Mini hotel and Tea stall	4	2,00,000	32
Flour mill and wet grinding	3	9,00,000	12
Jaggary	2	6,00,000	20
Fertilizer shop	3	3,00,000	9
Cattle rearing	3	3,00,000	15

Source: Self compilation.

farming functioning at Eachankottai near Thanjavur. Most of the petty shops are run by entrepreneurs who have education upto plus two level. Mini hotel and tea stall, flourmill and wet grinding are inherited business. Most of the women entrepreneurs were compelled to undertake the business due to mismanagement and sudden demise of their family members who had managed the business. Jaggary units are run by women entrepreneurs in Papanasam and Thiruvaiyaru taluk. Most of the jaggary units located nearer to sugarcane field. Women entrepreneurs in jaggary units took too much strain in extracting works from the workers. Fertilizer shops are run by educated women. At present, this business was affected due to poor monsoon and fall in agricultural operations. Cattle rearing are owned by old women and they managing the cattle farm with the help of child labourers which is against the norms of ILO.

Women entrepreneurs are facing certain problems during initial and current operations. Inadequate credit is the major problem. In capturing the market they have to face a stiff competition due to the commonly prevailing gender bias. The lack of confidence on the part of customers in a women's ability posses a threat in capturing the market. The exploitation of the society and the middlemen taking the weakness of women for granted also makes them defected in collecting the money. The gender difference sometimes does not allow men to work under women. The flexibility of the women is taken as a weak point and the labourers exploit them.

Lack of Finance

The biggest problem is finance or capital. Usually women do not have sufficient savings of their own to start business. They do not have collateral securities. So they are unable to get the financial assistance from the financial institutions easily. Only few women entrepreneurs availed loan from commercial banks.

Self Help Group for women were organized in village areas. Even the existing Self Help Group in villages are interested in money lending to the needy people at an exorbitant rate of interest and hence, completely deviating from the purpose of starting "Self Help Group".

Lack of Entrepreneurial Skills

Their inexperience, wrong selection of the project and inability to control the labourers are the hurdles for the women entrepreneurs to overcome. The inheritance compelled women entrepreneurs to enter into a business which is not liked by them.

Dual Role

When a woman wants to emerge as an entrepreneur, she has to discharge the household duties first and then to run the enterprise. The duel role makes the entrepreneur to devote less time for work. They feel frustrated because they need to spare their energy both towards business as well as domestic affairs. Some women entrepreneurs are ought to bear the expense of spend thrift husband because of social necessity.

Gender Bias

The male members of the family find fault with women entrepreneurs and reluctant to extend co-operation. This makes women entrepreneurs unhappy. The customers, traders and employees deny their co-operation to women entrepreneurs which leads to the problem of finding good market for their products.

Inability in Capturing Market

In experience, gender bias, the inability to move from one place to another cause problems in capturing the market. The gender bias underestimate the quality of product produced and service rendered by women.

Mobility

For socio-psychological reasons women do not want to leave their homes, unless they are compelled members and others. The non-cooperation of family members and exploitation by others make her face difficulties in running the enterprise.

The insincerity of the workers, disobedience of the labourers due to gender bias, attitude of the society also affect the performance of entrepreneurs. Technical and skilled workers moved to other units without giving any intimation to the women entrepreneurs.

Some educated girls in villages want to start units in tailoring, petty shop, fertilizer shop because they consider other units such as producing food products, milk farming, cattle rearing etc., as inferior. They think that manufacturing pickles, vadagam, appalam, rearing of cattle, managing milk farming are meant only for the illiterate persons.

Support Schemes Offered to Women Entrepreneurs in Tamil Nadu

In order to encourage women entrepreneurs many support schemes and special schemes were introduced in Tamil Nadu. They are as follows:

1. Small Industries and Service Institute.
2. Tamil Nadu Corporation for Development of Women Ltd.
3. Mahalir Kazhagam

4. Voluntary Organizations
   (a) Social Life Animation India (SOLAI)
   (b) Kovai Magalir Mandram (Komagal)

Special Schemes for Women Entrepreneurs in Tamil Nadu

1. Subsidy
2. District Industries Centre
3. Training Institutions
4. Sri Sakthi Yojana by the SBI
5. Priyadharshini Yojana by the Bank of India
6. Self Help Group for women started as a joint venture of the IOB and the social life animation of India movement.
7. Centre for Entrepreneurship Development for Women by the Canara Bank.
8. Mahila Udhayam Nidhi and Mahila Vikas Nidhi
9. Prime Minister Rozger Yojana (PMRY).

The women entrepreneur's in Thanjavur district (excepted few) are not aware of the support schemes and special schemes offered by the State and Central Government and Banks mainly because of ignorance. The government should give more attention for the promotion of business conducted by women. Now-a-days it is an urgent necessity, in the world of liberalization, privatization and globalisation, and for the raise of per-capita income, standard of life of family, women contribution is very essential. They can contribute for the financial improvement of their family directly and for the improvement of the nation indirectly.

References

1. Adarsh Kumari Sharma, Women Entrepreneurship in India (A case study of leading women entrepreneurs in India), *A Survey of Research in Commerce and Management,* 1994.

2. Anima Sen, "Problems and Potentials of Women Entrepreneurs: An Indian Perspective", Heptulla Najma (ed), *Reforms for Women, Future: Options,* Oxford & IBH Publication, New Delhi, 1992.

3. Bharathi, T.P.J., "Women Entrepreneurs in Salem District—A Success Story", *Mysore Economic Review,* 1991.

4. Gupta, C.B. and Srinivasan, M.P., *Entrepreneurial Development,* Sultan Chand and Sons, New Delhi, 1993.

5. Mythili, S., Women Entrepreneurs in Nagapattinam District—A Multi-dimensional Study, Bharathidasan University, 1998.

Magazines

Express Magazine

India Today

Times of India.

Development of Women Entrepreneurs in Rural India

S. Raju

Introduction

After Second World War, Women have been taken out of their traditional occupation to take up jobs out of homes. Of late the entrepreneurial world is also open to the women folk. While some higher middle income women of urban areas undertake small scale industry in the home making chalk, agarbathis or cleaning powder to keep up with their neighbour-hood, others become owners of small units due to the sudden demise of the head of the family.

Strategies for Developing Status of Woman Entrepreneurship

The most important means of achieving improvement in the status of woman employment is either low or on decline, should be identified and initiated to promote additional avenues for employment. Efforts are to be made to offer employment for woman in the co-operative activities like public distributive system, co-operative dairies, social forestries etc.

Various Assistance Programme

Entrepreneurship does not differentiate the sex. We know all types of assistance and various facilities offered to the entrepreneurs. These equally apply to women entrepreneurs also. However, certain additional facilities (or) incentives are offered to women entrepreneurs to motivate them and to bring them in the mainstream of industrial development.

Small Industrial Development Organisation (SIDO)

The SIDO through a network of Small Industries Service Institutes (SISI) throughout the country conduct the Entrepreneurial Development Programmes (EDP) exclusively for women entrepreneurs. These programmes aim at developing entrepreneurial traits and qualities among women and enable them to identify entrepreneurial opportunities, acquire basic knowledge and skills on enterprise building and the procedures of taking up small scale industries.

The SISI's provide technical consultancy and guidance to the entrepreneurs in right selection of an enterprise, preparation of feasibility reports, availability of plant and machinery and raw-materials and their sources of supply and how to avail assistance for finance and other inputs needed by an entrepreneur.

Technical Assistance

Considering development of women entrepreneurship as top priority, systematic efforts are made to provide credit and technical assistance. Which technical assistance is provided by the developmental agencies like Small Industries Service Institute (SISI), Technical Consultancy Organisations (TCO's) etc various women's organizations provide as a focal point for co-ordinating the activities.

Women Entrepreneur Cell of Indian Bank

Indian Bank was probably the first commercial bank to set up an exclusive cell for women entrepreneurs manned by trained lady officers. The role of the cell is to act as a catalyst and co-ordinating agency for promoting women entrepreneurship. The cell provides counselling assistance to women to choose products for manufacture and services make right investment decisions and also provide information on various requirements for running a business.

The National Small Industries Corporation Ltd. (NSIC)

The NSIC, which is a Govt. of India undertaking, has greatly been responsible for development of SSI sector. The hire purchase scheme of NSIC provides preferential treatment to women entrepreneurs. While the earnest money required from entrepreneurs for supply of machines is 20 per cent of the value in non backward areas, it is only 15 per cent for women entrepreneurs for machines valued upto Rs. 5 lakhs on timely payment of installments, the normal effective rate of payment is 13½ per cent. There is also lower service charges. NSIC also conducts Entrepreneurs and Enterprise building programmes for women.

IDBI Assistance Scheme for Women Entrepreneurs

The small scale industry covering broad spectrum of industrial units in small, tiny, village and cottage sectors occupies an important position in the industrial structure of the country. The Industrial Development Bank of India (IDBI) has been extending assistance to this sector on priority basis and a special scheme has been drawn up for assistance to women entrepreneurs subsequent to setting up of the Small Industries Development Fund.

IDBI Schemes of Training and Extension Service for Women Entrepreneurs

The programmes for training and extension services for women entrepreneurs will be organized by IDBI through designated or approved agencies independently and/in association with other development agencies like Entrepreneurship Development Institute of India, Technical Consultancy Organisation (TCO's) Central/State Social Welfare Boards and KVIC (Khadi and Village Industries Commissions) etc.

Generally the financial assistance to the training and development agencies would cover expenditure for items like rental for the training centres, boarding and lodging course material, industry or market visits, consultancy, post training follow-up and escort services. The total amount of subsidy from IDBI for such service would be a maximum of Rs. 10,000/- per beneficiary.

The training/promotional agency will maintain separate accounts showing details of expenditure in respect of each approved programme and submit to IDBI statement of expenditure in the prescribed form and evaluation report in respect of each sponsored programme within 4 weeks of its conclusion.

Other Schemes for IDBI's Refinance Assistance to Women Entrepreneurs

Eligibility

All projects in SSI sector (including Cottage Village and Tiny Industry) promoted and managed by women entrepreneurs will be eligible to get assistance under the scheme.

Promoters' Contribution

The minimum promoters' contribution would be 12.5 per cent of the project cost for units set up in category "A" (backward districts) and 15 per cent of the project cost in all other cases irrespective of location. Debt-Equity Ratio 3:1.

Rate of Interest

Uniform 12.5 per cent per annum with re-finance from IDBI at 9 per cent p.a. to the lending institutions.

Extent of Re-finance

It is 100 per cent of the loan amount for SFC's if covered under Automatic Refinance Schemes (ARS) and 85 per cent if the proposal comes under NRS. For projects setup in 'A' category backward districts the refinance is 90 per cent. In the case of banks the extent is 75 per cent of the loan amount both under ARS and NRS.

Security

Relaxation in security margin is considered by SFC's/ SID's where considered necessary.

Guarantee Cover

Whereever applicable loans to women entrepreneurs will be covered under the credit guarantee scheme of DIC GC. (District Industries Centre for Guarantee Cover).

Mahila Udyam Nidhi (MUN) Scheme

Apart from the above, IDBI has introduced a special schemes for women entrepreneurs like Mahila Udyam Nidhi Scheme (MUN) with a corpus fund of Rs. 5 crores to provide seed capital assistance to new women entrepreneurs in SSI sector.

Women entrepreneurs owning and managing an enterprise with a minimum financial stake of 51 per cent of the equity are eligible under the scheme. All new projects in the small scale sector set up by women entrepreneurs, preferably trained under on Entrepreneurship Development Programme are eligible for assistance provided the cost of the project does not exceed Rs. 10 lakhs.

The operating institutions are the state financial corporations (SFC's) or State Industrial Development Corporation (SIDCO's) who act as agent of IDBI for sanction disbursement and recovery of soft seed capital assistance. Under the scheme SFC's/SIDC's will sanction seed capital assistance—simultaneously term loan assistance for the project after satisfying its viability and the need for seed capital assistance. The credit risk irrespective of soft seed capital assistance borne by IDBI, Mahila Udyam Nidhi.

The Scheme stipulates that the promoter's contributions of 10 per cent of the project cost and that the debt equality ratio should be 3:1. The quantum of assistance is the amount of meet the gap in equity after taking into account promoter's contributions to the project subject to a minimum of 15 per cent. A nominal service charge of 1 per cent p.a. is levied of the seed capital assistance. In case the financial position and profitability of the unit so warrant, a higher rate of service charge but not exceeding the normal rate of interest on term loans could be applied.

Specified Due Date

The seed capital assistance is repayable over a period of 10 years including an initial moratorium not exceeding 5 years. The seed capital assistance is unsecured and no security/collateral is needed from the borrowers.

Suggestions

Most of the State/UT Governments have introduced incentive schemes which include seed/margin money contribution, subsidy in preparation of feasibility report. Sales tax exemption or deferment, exemption from octroi duty, 'subsidy on power tariff, subsidy on rent, price preference, raw materials assistance etc. These incentives are available to women entrepreneurs as well apart from special/additional assistance offered to them.

Conclusion

In India women entrepreneurship development schemes are introduced by every Government in large, but the operation and out reach of such launches are unknown to the public in general and to the women folk in particular. To overcome this problem and to improve women entrepreneurship in India the government has to conduct out reach programmes towards women of the middle class and lower middle class women group. If the out reach programmes are not satisfactory the government have to conduct counseling among the women which will help them to come out successful without fear. Because fear among the women is a big hurdle for these kinds of development.

References

1. S.B. Srivastava
2. Dr. V. Balu.

Growth of Rural Women Entrepreneurs in the Union Territory of Pondicherry

Dr. K. Sivaloganathan

Introduction

Women in our country have been given a prestigious place. As a mask of respect to women, the earth and rivers are named after women. In the world population half of the population are women. Women are competing successfully with men despite the social economic and psychological constraints. An international labour organisation report in 1980 stated that women are 50 per cent of the world population do the 2/3 of the world's work hours, receive 10 per cent of world's income and own less than 1 per cent of the world property. With regard to India, women constitute 60 per cent of the rural unemployed and 56 per cent of the total unemployed. Entrepreneurship is traced out as an extension of their kitchen activities to pickles powder (masala) and pappad manufacturing. At present, with growing awareness and spread of education over the years, women have started engrosing the modern activities like engineering, electronics and energy. The state of Kerala where the literacy among women is highest in India, provide a good example of entrepreneurship among women.

An attempt is made in this empirical study to identity the "opportunities available for women rural entrepreneurs in the Union Territory of Pondicherry.

General

The Union Territory of Pondicherry is constituted out of four erstwhile French establishments of Pondicherry, Karaikal, Mahe and Yanam. It is interesting to note that Pondicherry is located about 170 kms. south of Chennai. Karaikal lies about 150 kms further down south, near Nagapattinam. Mahe lies on the western ghats surrounded by Kerala and is about 652 kms away from Pondicherry and Yanam is about 840 kms northeast of Pondicherry near Kakinada in Andhra Pradesh. Pondicherry was declared as an industrially backward area in 1971 and many incentives like central investment subsidy, power subsidy, sales tax holiday, etc., were extended by Government of Pondicherry to promote industrial development. Government of Pondicherry also provides very good infrastructural facilities of roads, electricity and water supply. Above all Pondicherry has very informal work culture where all Government executives and even Ministers are easily approachable. Pondicherry provides a peaceful and quality work force with no hassles of trade unions. And all this has made Pondicherry a heaven for existing and new industrial units.

Industrial Estates

Six industrial estates are presently in existence and additional industrial parks are being planned. A Techno Park at Thirubuvanai, Pondicherry is ready and being allotted. A Growth Centre at Polagam in Karaikal is being set up. Also an informational technology park (Pondy Technopolics) at Pondicherry Engineering College Campus at Kalapet in Pondicherry is ready and being allotted.

Opportunities

For this empirical study, a sample of 123 women entrepreneurs has been selected based on convenience sampling method. A questionnaire was adopted to know the opportunities available for the women entrepreneurs in this region. The opportunities identified are finance, procurement of raw material, cooperation from the labourers, marketing and assistances from the Government.

1. *Finance*

The study revealed regarding financial assistance that a major source has been notified from the PIPDIC which consists 62 respondents (50.40 per cent). It is followed by 29 of them, who have approached District Industrial Centre, (DIC) which is 23.58 per cent. 23 entrepreneurs have got finance from friends and relatives which is 18.70 per cent and remaining entrepreneurs have mobilised from private source which is 4.88 per cent, share capital contribution is 6 which makes 44 per cent vide Table 26.1.

Table 26.1. Source of Finance

Sl. No.	Source	No. of respondents	Percentage (%)
1.	Friends & Relatives	23	18.70
2.	DIC	29	23.58
3.	Govt.	62	50.40
4.	Share Capital	3	2.44
5.	Private Source	6	4.88
	Grand Total	**123**	**100**

Source: Primary data.

2. *Procurement of Raw Material*

The raw material with reference to its supply is shown in Table 26.2. The table indicates that 37 of the entrepreneurs i.e. 30.08 per cent buy the raw material from outside the state but within the country. It is followed by 33 entrepreneurs (26.83) who buy it within the state. 26 entrepreneurs (21.14 per cent) who buy it locally. Only 14 (11.38 per cent) of the entrepreneurs who buy outside the country. It should be noted here that these entrepreneur import raw material from other countries. However in general, majority of the entrepreneurs get regular supply of raw materials.

Table 26.2. Place of Purchase of Raw Material

Sl. No.	Source	No. of respondents	Percentage (%)
1.	Locally Available	26	21.14
2.	Within the State	33	26.83
3.	Outside the State but within country	37	30.8
4.	Outside the country	14	11.38
5.	Own arrangements	11	8.94
6.	Other ways	2	1.63
	Grand Total	**123**	**100**

Source: Primary data.

3. *Cooperation from Labourers*

It is an additional blessing for an entrepreneur who gets support and cooperation from employees. In consolidation 112 entrepreneurs (91 per cent) have got cooperation and help from the labourers in carrying out their ventures. The non cooperation is felt only by 11 entrepreneurs which comes to only 9 per cent. The Government is providing all the welfare measures and reasonable wage system so that the workers are secured and happy vide Table 26.3.

Table 26.3. Cooperation of Employees

Sl. No.	Source	No. of respondents	Percentage (%)
1.	Yes	112	91.06
2.	No	11	8.94
	Grand Total	**123**	**100**

Source: Primary data.

4. *Marketing*

The geographical coverage of market is one of the factor which would later influence the possibility of expanding the market. Table 26.4 shows the location of market. It is clear from the table that 29 of the entrepreneurs have local market (23.58 per cent). 52 of them have market within the state

(42.28 per cent). 42 of them sell the product outside the state but within the country (34.15 per cent). The Government takes all the steps to arrange for the marketing of the goods of the entrepreneurs. They provide financial assistance also for the interim period. Besides this the Govt. also arranges for local level and national level exhibitions and Trade Favis for promoting their sales.

Table 26.4. Marketing of Products

Sl. No.	Marketing place	No. of respondents	Percentage (%)
1.	Locally	29	23.58
2.	Within the state	52	42.28
3.	Outside the state but within the country	42	34.15
	Grand Total	**123**	**100**

Source: Primary data.

5. *Government Assistances*

The statistical data relating to Government Assistance can be seen from the Table 26.5. For the success of an

Table 26.5. Government Assistance

Sl. No.	Factors	No. of respondents	Percentage (%)
1.	Large amount of loan and simply procedure	33	26.83
2.	Increase the range of marketing	8	6.50
3.	Procurement of inputs	18	14.63
4.	Efficient utilization of inputs	2	6.50
5.	Provision of the right kind of education and training to increase efficiency	28	22.77
6.	Subsidies	5	4.08
	Grand Total	**123**	**100.00**

Source: Primary data.

enterprise the entrepreneur has to explain not only their initiative and hard work but also the cooperation and help from Government and Non-Government agencies. It is evident that higher amount of loans and simple procedures takes the major share in assisting the entrepreneurs as 33 respondents (26.83 per cent) approach bank for help. The subsidies offer a supporting hand to 28 entrepreneurs (22.77 per cent). 20 entrepreneurs (16.26 per cent) provide the right kind of education which will breed industrial entrepreneurship. 18 entrepreneurs (14.63 per cent) are getting help from Government in procurement of inputs commonly needed by the small firms 8 of the entrepreneurs (6.50 per cent) are getting help from Government to increase the range of marketing and efficient utilisation of inputs.

Conclusion

It is evident from the findings that the Govt. of Pondicherry is encouraging the emergence of entrepreneurs in the region. Regarding the capital the enterprises are financed adequately by DIC, PIPDIC, SIDBI and commercial banks. The Govt. also liberally provides licences, variety of concessions, subsidies incentives and all other infrastructure facilities. Thus the development of entrepreneurship in general and rural women entrepreneur in particular in Pondicherry region is quite encouraging and satisfactory.

Challenges for Women Entrepreneurs in Rural India

Dr. V. Madasamy

Introduction

The concept of '*Women Entrepreneur*' is becoming a global phenomenon today. All over the world, women are playing a vital role in the business community. In India, however women have made a comparatively late entry into the business scenario mainly due to the orthodox and traditional socio-cultural environment. Though they are enjoying a special status in the society, women entrepreneurs face various problems in the process of establishing, developing and running their enterprises in the 21st century.

The Concept of Women Entrepreneur

Women entrepreneurs may be defined as the women or a group of women who initiate, organise and operate a business enterprise. Women are expected to innovate, imitate or adopt an economic activity to be called *Women Entrepreneurs*.

The Government of India has defined a woman entrepreneur as an "enterprise owned and administered by women entrepreneurs having a minimum financial interest of 51 per cent of the share capital and giving at least 50 per cent of the employment generated in the enterprise to women".

Functions of Women Entrepreneurs

According to Frederick Harbison, like a male entrepreneur, a woman entrepreneur has five functions: These are:

1. Explore the prospects of starting new enterprises
2. Undertaking of risks and the handling of economic and non-economic uncertainties
3. Introduction of new innovations or imitation of successful ones in existence
4. Co-ordination, administration and control
5. Supervision and providing leadership in all aspects of the business

Basic Traits of Women Entrepreneurs

Normally the women entrepreneurs, who prefer to start an enterprise should have the following traits:

1. Accept challenges
2. Adventurous
3. Ambitious
4. Conscientious
5. Full of drive
6. Educated
7. Enthusiastic
8. Hard working
9. Keen to learn and imbibe
10. Patient
11. Intelligent
12. Motivated
13. Skilful
14. Studious
15. Optimistic

Though women entrepreneurs in rural areas are having the above said qualities to a certain extent, they are facing some problems. The greatest deterrent to women entrepreneurs is that they are women.

The main problems faced by the women entrepreneurs in recent days are:

1. Financial constraints
2. Over dependence on intermediaries
3. Scarcity of raw materials
4. Intense competition
5. High cost of production
6. Low mobility
7. Family ties
8. Social attitudes
9. Lack of education
10. Absence of ambition for achievement.

The above problems and stumbling blocks, which are most commonly mentioned by women entrepreneurs or prospective women entrepreneurs, are elaborately discussed under:

Access to Material Resources/Capital

- Credit/Financial services
- Land/Property/Assets
- Collateral/Security for accessing credit
- Technologies: know-how plus Machinery, Tool, Equipment etc.
- Raw materials: regularity of supply, quality, infrastructural links etc.

Access to Market and Market Information

Marketing strategies/Feasibility of a product in the market/trade-links/Competing effectively.

Access to Variety of Technical and Skills Training

Technical/vocational/managerial/organisation, financial, personnel, production process, self-confidence building, negotiation skills, assertiveness.

Access to Business Related Services

Business counselling and follow-up services after training or counselling.

Access to Information in All Aspects

Marketing, credit facilities and financial services, technology, training and education.

Legal Issues

- Discriminating laws, e.g., Property Rights, Inheritance Laws which deprive women of capital (or) collateral/securities.
- Police harassment on grounds of certain regulations exist (e.g. Licence requirements); restrictions to operate in certain areas (e.g., residential versus commercial areas).

Gender Issues

Mixed with socio-cultural factors, the concern of the women's place and their role within the family and society; the perception of family and society's expectation on women etc and she is the care-taker of the family, and not the bread-winner. Her primary role is in the family sphere, and not in the public sphere. Even if the reality is often different, these social norms and expectations, limit women's options; they limit women's mobility and acceptability in the business world; they determine the approach of bankers/credit institutions to women; they determine the support or approval by family members; they affect the self-esteem and self-confidence; they influence the nature and quality of work experience which women "are allowed to" acquire; and the educational level and level of professional experience also have the influence on women entrepreneurs.

Ways and Means

The above problems of women entrepreneurs can be solved by adoption of the following ways and means:

- As far as development of women entrepreneurship is concerned there is no dearth of entrepreneurial talent among women, what is needed is to develop a clear entrepreneurial attitude;

  Natural talents, aptitudes, capabilities can be multiplied through training programmes to develop self-confidence, self-esteem, assertiveness, courage and risk;

- Emergence of women entrepreneurship in a society depends to a great extent on the economic, social, religious, cultural and psychological factors prevailing in the society;

  Development of women entrepreneurship needs proper environment and for their healthy and sound entrepreneurial climate are to be created;

- Training programmes should be designed in such manners that women entrepreneurs can benefit out of their strengths and overcome their weaknesses;
- Training programmes should provide special assistance for selection of procedure/service so that women entrepreneur can be in a position to perceive and respond to various profitable opportunities;
- A good management ground is needed to women entrepreneurs for their better performance in their enterprises.
- There is an urgent need to educate women for taking up entrepreneurship and for stressing benefits of entrepreneurship. This awareness can be achieved through conferences, seminar, special training programmes, refresher courses, awareness camps and other related activities;
- Success stories of women entrepreneurs from varied backgrounds should be published through textbook

of schools, and colleges and possible media should be used to project these role models effectively;

- Efforts are needed to remove the inferiority complex and to make women more confident about themselves;
- Efforts should be made to locate entrepreneurial potentialities amongst housewives and opportunities should be provided to them;
- Governmental and other Non-Governmental Organisations should make efforts to provide facilities in the form of child care institutions like crèches, nurseries and child-care facilities to solve the problems of childcare;
- Illiteracy has been major barrier for women entrepreneurship development. Education develops the personality. Educated individuals can take independent decisions. Through education, knowledge and proper exposure, potentialities of women can be increased. For developing entrepreneurial talent and preventing the possibility of industrial failure, the financial and other agencies should conduct training programmes before sanctioning and disbursing business assistance;
- Illiterate women should be trained modern techniques and latest trends in activities like sewing, dairy, bakery, spinning, weaving, leather products, screen-printing, etc. So that productive utilisation of their time and capacities can take place. More over, there is a tremendous scope for agro-based industries like animal husbandry, poultry, dairy, food processing, sericulture, agriculture, horticulture etc;
- Women generally do not have their own money to invest. Further, they do not have courage and risk bearing capacity, which is needed for successful entrepreneurship. In such cases, women with similar interests and similar economic background can form

groups so as to share risk, knowledge and investment;

- Women should be encouraged to form co-operative societies exclusively for women. It is the responsibility of the co-operative sector of the State Government to provide all the necessary help and guidance. Then only with the help of co-operative endeavour, women entrepreneurship will flourish;
- At district level, a separate organisation can be formed so as to take into all aspects of women entrepreneurship development. This organisation can help women entrepreneurs in fulfilling their requirements of financial assistance, marketing aid, obtaining subsidies, concessions, technical know-how, raw material assistance, conduct of market surveys to assess feasibility, counselling, follow up guidance etc.

Conclusion

For stimulating entrepreneurship among women significant efforts have to be made by a number of departments of Central and State Government in terms of offering incentives/benefits. Even the industrial policies, five-year plans emphasize the promotion of women entrepreneurship.

A variety of programmes have been undertaken by a multitude of organisations with the intention of stimulating women entrepreneurship. When such kind of support is extended, certainly there will be spurt in the number of rural women entrepreneurs to future economic prosperity of our rural based nation.

Financial and Social Constraints of Rural Women Entrepreneurs

S. Senthil Sreenivasan

Introduction

Women Entrepreneurship in India is at nascent stage. Empowerment of women and their economic participation is vital for a country for its development and global recognition. India, a rich land of various resources has failed to achieve economic growth due to numerous factors. Among the major disturbing factors, poor women entrepreneurism is the most important factor, which has to be addressed. Rural India is poor in economic means, but not of human capital, ability and commitment. Indian economic strength is determined by the rural economy, which is poor in two aspects, namely financial and social. These two aspects are to be considered and issues relating to this are to be analysed and solved.

Rural women are renowned segment of our society with high degree of sincerity, commitment and hard work. Worthwhile to mention is their undermined capability. If this section of society are recognized and motivated to enter the threshold of entrepreneurship, it is certain that our country's economy can be strengthened financially and socially. Rural women hesitate to take up entrepreneurship, because of two major constraints namely social and financial. The former and the latter play equal role in containing the spirit of entrepreneurship among rural women.

Strength

Rural women population is vibrant and can move mountains. They possess eloquent qualities, which are absent among men population. They are highly superior in the following qualities:

(a) Competency to handle critical situations and issues;

(b) High degree of diligence and developable skill;

(c) Unpredictable commitment to work and achieve objectives;

(d) Innovative methods in operating work;

(e) Greater degree of sincerity.

Issue

In spite of the above qualities, lack of recognition of, and encouragement to women is the formidable reason for poor development in rural women entrepreneurship. Identical and dimensional reasons are status, culture, acceptancy, perception attitude and customs. These are the social issues and act as impediments for growth of women entrepreneurship. The secondary constraint is lack of financial resources, few and less incentives and lack of moral support. There are minor issues which are with lesser intensity, like family background, communication skills, innovative thinking, educational quality, perception, foreseeing ability, business ethics, quick decision making capability etc. Proper and adequate measures can remove these small and meager drawbacks. But the two main constraints finance and society affects the rural women in starting new business ventures.

Problems

The social constraints are the exhaustive cause for non-development of entrepreneurship ability of rural women. If social constraints are eliminated or wiped off, then the possibilities of women entrepreneurship in rural India is quite formidably near the goalpost.

The social constraints are the following:

1. The gender bias, prevailing in all types of communities;
2. Traditional customary practices and unfructiable limiting boundaries;
3. Lack in social mobility, freedom and liberation;
4. Dominance of men over the women;
5. Cultural bottlenecks which relies on centuries old practice;
6. Poor recognition by the society;
7. Lack of self-confidence and motivation forces.

Apart from social constraints there is a second factor, which is dominant and violent, namely the financial resource that is much inevitable ingredient for business. The lack or shortage or non-availability of the funds will no doubt lead to crisis.

The rural segment does have lesser financial support and assistance compared to the urban section. Especially, the women population of rural regions is not assisted with financial requirement by banks, financial institutions or private sector bankers. The meager numbers of banks operate in rural areas and restrictive policies relating to loans and advances of such banks in rural areas are the related factors for sluggishness in lending operations. In addition the infrastructure of banks are inadequate to impart with the financial services. The major limitation is the financial policies of the banks in sanctioning of advances to rural women. To sum-up, the financial hindrances are:

1. Fewer numbers of banks in rural areas;
2. Restrictive financial lending policy of banks;
3. Limited operations and schemes of the lending institutions;
4. Unfavourable Governmental policy and insufficient supportive measures;

5. Lack of information about the schemes of finance available.

Comments

The competence of rural women is underestimated in India. When it is accepted that *"behind a successful man, there is a women"*, why it is believed that women does not possess enough competence in becoming entrepreneurs?

The perception and attitudes of the people are to be refreshed with changing business scenarios and enormous developments in developed societies and communities.

The culture and customs are the major bottlenecks in development of entrepreneurial skills among women. The system of Indian culture restricts or abandons the women to enter the business field. Traditional and unethical constituents of culture should be scaled down and replaced with high profile principles and practices.

No compromisory words can be substantiated to undermine the entrepreneurship abilities or innovative ideas of rural women. They possess and can learn more than what successful men entrepreneurs have accomplished.

The governments should evolve with new policies and various schemes to rural women, encouraging them to reap the business opportunities. Infact, the Rozgar Yozana scheme of the Central Government was a successful step towards creating jobs and income for rural people, similar and viable schemes of this nature should be announced by the governments so as to make the rural women to come out with new innovative ideas and practices, this will lead them to become good and enabled entrepreneurs.

Conclusion

A high determination is to be inducted in the mind and thoughts of rural women, enabling them to reap the superlative hidden qualities which certainly will lead to their success in life, livelihood, status, earnings and social recognition. It is unnecessary to wait for a transition time for motivating rural women to take up entrepreneurship. It is universally accepted principle that conservation leads to excellence. Women are renowned persons of conservation. They are capable segments of the society who can care for conservative policies and successful actions. These rural women are more intelligent, capable, bright, experienced, hard working, just flat-out capable group on the Indian economic scenario and the world as the whole.

Impact of Micro Credit Programmes on Rural Women

Haji Dr. M. Sheik Mohamed
N. Arul Prakash

Introduction

Women groups and NGOs initiated micro credit programmes at local levels as one component of the development strategy to empower poor women. But now a days micro credit is no longer a localized activity. For banks and financial institutions micro credit offers new avenues of profit making since interest rates range from 20 to 40 per cent and repayment rates are over 90 per cent, far above commercial lending.

The most common criterion used for measuring the success of micro credit programmes is the loan repayment rate. The loan repayment rate is very high compared to commercial lending but this does not explain the qualitative impact of such programmes in terms of increasing flows of income, levels of employment and sustainability of businesses. Since the lenders are primarily concerned with repayment of loans, vital issues related to the quality and wider socio-economic impact of such loans have not been given due attention.

Impact of Micro Credit Programmes

The recent studies on impact of micro credit programmes run by Grameen Bank of Bangladesh, one of the pioneers of micro credit, reveal that workers and peer group members put pressure on women borrowers for timely repayment, rather than devising a strategy of collective responsibility and borrower empowerment, as originally envisaged by the bank. Under such pressure, many women borrowers maintain their regular repayment schedules through loan recycling which ultimately increases the debt liability of the borrower. The increased debt liability, in turn, aggravates family tension and produces new forms of social dominance and often violence against women borrowers.

Empirical studies reveal that it is not always the poorest of poor women who get the credit. Those with sizeable income and assets often corner the biggest chunk of credit. Further studies have also reported that much of the credit is used by poor women to meet consumption needs rather than investment in businesses. The growing dependence of micro credit institutions on donors is a matter for serious concern. There are very few instances where micro credit institutions have become sustainable without the support of donors. This is despite the fact that most micro lenders charge relatively higher interest rates in the range of 12 to 36 per cent. Therefore, a proper regulatory framework under which micro-lenders should function is needed in India.

Women Entrepreneurs

Advocates of micro credit programmes view poverty as a cash flow problem and seek its solutions through credit and income generation programmes. Poverty particularly that of women, cannot be defined only interms of cash flow since it has strong linkages with imaginable distribution of resources, unequal power relations, illiteracy, lower wages, cuts in developmental spending and anti-poor macro-economic policies that disproportionately affect poor women. It also needs to be emphasized that micro credit is not a substitute for social sector spending and anti poverty programmes.

In the rural context, women's control over ownership of land can play an important role not only in economic betterment but also in terms of social and political empowerment as land is a symbol of political power and social status. Further micro credit programmes have to be visualized in the context of the new global economic order in liberalization, privatisation and globalisation policies which have led to job losses in the formal sector, decline in social sector spending and growing unemployment. In this scenario, the last option left for poor women is self-employment, which micro credit aims to promote.

But poor women are placed at a disadvantageous position in the market. How can the products of poor women compete with those of big business and transactional corporations which not only have strong financial backing but also spend millions on advertising, brand-selling and marketing. Until and unless poor women are provided access to market information, technology, management and marketing skills, their economic ventures will remain uncompetitive.

Conclusion

Since the efficacy of micro credit programmes is not independent of other developmental interventions, it could at best be one of the components of a wider developmental agenda.

Women Entrepreneurship for Rural Industrialisation

R. Jegadeeswaran

Introduction

Entrepreneurship is a complex phenomenon viewed differently by different people. Some think of entrepreneurs primarily as "Innovators" with dynamism in their approach. Entrepreneurial potential can be found and developed irrespective of socio-economic backgrounds, location, sex, age, education and experience. It is therefore, necessary to generate and transmit this feeling among the unemployed youth to sow the seeds of Entrepreneurship. The educated unemployed youth are to be motivated to become efficient and successful entrepreneurs.

As the world moves, however haltingly toward a global economy, the barriers among nations will gradually dissolve. At present, we need such entrepreneurs who tend to tackle the unknown; they do things in new and different ways; they weave old ideas into new patterns; they offer more solutions than excuses. Entrepreneurship is the capacity for innovation and calibre to introduce innovative techniques in the business operations. The entrepreneur creates new opportunities for success.

Entrepreneurship in India

The Indian economy was literally stagnant in the pre-independence period. To set this anomaly right, after independence, Indian planners launched a series of five year plans at pooling our scarce resources together and through that built up infrastructure such as major core industries, irrigation and power projects, etc.

In a developing country like India, the role of the entrepreneurs is supporting and backing up the governments effort to accelerate the harnessing of vast resources. The infrastructure that was built during the process has given rise to tremendous opportunities to the enterprises. It has helped people to set up various ventures putting to use various resource including men and material. The contribution of these private enterprises is quite significant both in terms of employment and national income.

Significance of Entrepreneur

Human agent lies at the center of the process, of economic development. According to Schumpter, entrepreneurs are the agents who provide economic leadership that distributes the initial conditions of the economy and causes dynamic changes. Hence the entrepreneur is an integral part of the strategy of industrialisation.

Systematic and organised nurturing of entrepreneurship would ultimately generate pressure on the existing, socio-economic and political institution, cultural attitudes, practices and values towards modernisation.

Women Entrepreneurs

Women who make half of the world's population can no more remain as ornamental, decorative pieces but a productive human resource and recognised as such with all their entitlement. The core of women empowerment framework can be viewed in terms of five levels of equality. The empowerment is an essential element of welfare, access, conscientisation, participation and control. The existing statistics states that, women's sex ratio, educational levels, health standards, maternal mortality rate, infant mortality rate and employment levels continue to be in a deplorable state.

Women are not provided with their basic minimum requirements as they are bonded with economic emancipation. Rural industrialisation is the only best alternative available to make the women empowered and stimulate the process of sustainable development.

The improvement in the status of women is successful only when they improve their skills and join the labour force. The gradual strengthening of women's position in the society can be seen by the fact that the Child Marriage Restraint Act has raised the minimum age for the marriage of girls to 21 years and that of boys to 23 years. "Literacy of women is an important key to improve upon health, nutrition and education in the family and in empowering women to participate in decision-making in society. Investing in formal and non-formal education and training for girls and women, with its exceptionally high social and economic return, has proved to be one of the best means of achieving sustainable development and economic growth that is both sustained and sustainable.

Objectives

The basic objectives underlying the development of rural industries:

1. To increase in the supply in manufactured goods;
2. To increase in the promotion of coital formation;
3. Creation of employment opportunity.

Rural industries constitute the key in the process of socio-economic transformation of underdevelopment social structures. Out of the total industrial employment in the country, about 80 per cent is provided by village and cottage industries. If the rural industries are well managed, rapid economic development will be possible in the country.

According to Schumpter an entrepreneur is one who introduces something new into the economy. In Indian context, entrepreneur is more an adapter or 'initiator' than a true innovator. Therefore, any woman who initiates, innovates or adopts an economic activity may be called woman entrepreneur.

Women Entrepreneurs in Rural Industries

In the development of rural industries, there should be a comprehensive, integrated approach. The authorities responsible for development of rural industries must take action simultaneously on the various components of the programmes especially in the case of women entrepreneurs. 50 per cent of the total population constitutes women, but women workers constitute only 16 per cent of total population. Out of this 16 per cent, 80 per cent remains engaged in unorganized sectors. Entrepreneurship among women is a recent phenomenon. Although the number of women entrepreneurs is on the increase proportionately it is small in comparison with those in the developed countries of the world.

Women should be actively involved in all the extension programmes at the village/grassroot level.

Many media programmes play a vital role in promoting the awareness about the latest know-how. Hence, more and more video films, television programmes, radio talks about rural and cottage industries programmes must be made and popularized widely.

Women should be trained in the income generating activities related to small and medium scale as well as cottage industries.

- Agro-processing industries
- Food processing
- Readymade garments
- Plastic goods
- Making pickles and readymade masalas
- Printing
- Leather goods
- Hotels and Restaurants
- Trading in wholesale and retail in finished goods

- Fruits and vegetables
- Services like beauty parlors and laundry embroidery making greeting cards
- Basket weaving
- Bidi making
- Fiber based industries/rope making
- Leaf cup and plate
- Sericulture, a romantic plants and perfumery
- Medicinal plants and herbal industry etc.

The various components of the development of rural industries are:

1. Identification of opportunities for rural industries.
2. Entrepreneurial skills
3. Financial support
4. Technical assistance
5. Procedures to facilitate procurement of quality raw material and equipment
6. Industrial training and development administration
7. Marketing support

Successful Women Entrepreneurship

The following are the important pre-requisites for women entrepreneurs to become successful.

1. *Strong determination*

Only independent and determined persons make successful entrepreneurs.

2. *Commitment*

The women entrepreneurs need ability to stick to her goal through thick and thin and should not get this to heart.

3. *Aggressiveness*

Aggressiveness, if positively used provides a thrust towards growth and achievement. Aggressive character helps in surviving in a male-dominated sphere of entrepreneurship.

4. *Hard work*

A woman needs to work much harder than a man. A total mental and physical involvement is needed especially when the woman happens to be the (kingpin) of her business. The burden in a woman entrepreneur is greater as she also has to bear the load of her household.

5. *Risk-bearing*

A woman entrepreneur should study the market situation, explore profitability in different lines of business, products, machinery, finance etc., before taking a final decision.

6. *Knowledge*

A thorough knowledge in every aspect of her business is needed. The manual skills and other talents constitute the secondary knowledge of her business and its environment would enable her to see and seize opportunities. She needs to update her knowledge.

7. *Administrative skills*

Woman entrepreneur should have a fundamental knowledge in all functional areas of business namely production, marketing, finance, personal accounting etc.

Initiatives and Efforts taken in India

1. The first national conference of women entrepreneurs held at New Delhi—1981 was a milestone in the history of women entrepreneurs.
2. The Seventh Five-year Plan contained a special chapter namely integration of women in development.
3. IDBI has been refinancing the financial assistance granted by the banks at 9 per cent p.a. in respect of projects undertaken by women entrepreneurs.

4. SIDBI has been conducting various programmes for the benefit of women entrepreneurs.
5. The commercial banks help entrepreneurship development by attenuating uncertainty and facilitating risk while making available the capital needed by the people for undertaking self employment activities.
6. SBI, one of the biggest commercial banks in India, to promote entrepreneur sanctioned Rs. 12,700 crore to small scale industries.
7. SBI in 1998 for bringing about technology upgradation of small and medium entrepreneurs has taken up 15 projects so far in India.
8. SBI corporate loan scheme, launched during 1999-2000, was well received by the entrepreneur clients and over Rs. 1500 crore of such loans were sanctioned to various entrepreneurs during the year 2000-01.
9. Nehru Rozgar Yojana: Under this scheme 75 per cent of funds are provided by banks and 25 per cent by women finance corporation. 20 per cent subsidy is given to women entrepreneurs.
10. Under Prime Minister's integrated urban poverty eradication programme woman finance corporation provides financial assistance to set up units which require capital less than Rs. 10 lakhs.
11. 3 opened of credit granted under IRDP is exclusively meant for rural women entrepreneurs.
12. A variety of programmes is being undertaken, and a multitude of institutions exist in private as well as public sectors for the cause of promoting women entrepreneurship.

Development of Women Entrepreneurs

1. Women have to be made compatible of both social and economical worlds and empower them towards self-confidence and self-reliance.

2. Successful women in the field of entrepreneurship have to help other women in starting and sustaining in their business whole-heartedly.
3. All women entrepreneurs should join together and form co-operative societies to see their industries run effectively.
4. Literacy levels of women have to be enhanced and education of women should be made compulsory.
5. Entrepreneurship education and training at all levels have to be introduced (from basic education to P.G. levels).
6. Promotion of women entrepreneurship as an important and valued component has to be taken care of.
7. Women entrepreneurship research and applications for time to time have to be documented.
8. Women should be made aware of various credit facilities, financial incentives and subsidies.
9. Women entrepreneurship to develop in the form of training skill upgradation, managerial skills, production and marketing along with health and nutrition, women and child welfare etc.
10. For effective sustainable development and technology transfer to women entrepreneurs, proper training based on scientific inputs, suitable product ideas, product identification, market survey, project formulation and necessary approvals from the government at the right time.

Conclusion

Women can prove their success in the field of rural industries through proper guidance and assistance. The women entrepreneurship development in the small sector particularly in villages can integrate than in the economic development of the country.

REFERENCES

1. Rural Industrialist M.S.P.
2. Women Entrepreneurs in the Informal sector, Study of Kerala.
3. Southern Economist Dect. 1999, Kisan World, varies issues.

Emerging Women Entrepreneurs in Rural India

S. Jothi Mani

Introduction

Mahatma Gandhiji underlined the importance of rural areas by saying that India lives in villages. The role of village and cottage industries in rural development is considered as vital as these are the very backbone of the Indian rural economic with 74 per cent of our population still living in rural areas. India is predominantly an *agrarian* society, this agriculture has provided much more employment opportunities in the village for rural youth and women.

Concept of Women Entrepreneurs

Women Entrepreneurs are the women or a group of women who initiate, organize and operate a business enterprise. The Government of India notes women entrepreneurs as

> "an enterprise owned and controlled by women saving a minimum financial interest of 51 per cent of the capital and giving at least 51 per cent of the employment generated in the enterprise to women".

Emerging Women Entrepreneurs

The emergence of women entrepreneur depends on religious environmental socio-economic and psychological factors it is grouped under "pull factors" and "push factors".

Pull factors refers to the urge in women to undertake a venture with an inclination to start a business.

Push factors refers women entering business, driven by financial need due to family circumstances.

Opportunities for Rural Women Entrepreneurs

It is most important to create a favourable atmosphere for a healthy development of women's entrepreneurship we have an example of Kerala, how they work in a favourable atmosphere since last two decades. In 1975-76 the number of industrial units run by women entrepreneurs in Kerala was 73. It has increased to 4190 industrial units in 1993-94. The women entrepreneurs in Kerala are now at the top as all industrial right readymade garments to high-tech computers.

Suitable Rural Entrepreneurial Activities for Women

Selection of suitable industry depends of existing women's entrepreneurial capabilities, family support, and locational advantage and availability of financial and raw material and other infrastructure facilities etc.

Handloom cottage industries, khadi and village industries are providing employment opportunities to women. Entrepreneurship started by women is no longer confined to conventional fields like embroidery, knitting and tailoring or 3P's pickles, powder, and pappad, but women are venturing now it to modern technological field or 3E's energy, electricity and electronics.

But now the scenario is changing fast with modernization, and development of education and business. Thus the opportunities of employment for women have increased drastically. Self employment opportunities are still popular among rural women, they can start poultry, dairy, piggeries, bee-keeping goatry, petty shop keeping match boxes, agarpathy, agriculture and allied operations and establish small units to produce sauce and other similar products in corrective way.

Potential Industrial Opportunities in Theni District

In Theni District we have wide potential industrial opportunities such as,

1. Cattle and poultry feed
2. Leather products (chapels and bags)
3. Agricultural farm implements
4. Bakery products
5. Manufacturing note books
6. Pickles and appalams
7. Herbal cultivation and processing
8. Mineral water plant
9. Extraction of cocount oil
10. Coir mat weaving
11. Mango fruit pulps, juices, jams and squashes
12. Turmeric powder
13. Instant food mix
14. Handlooms
15. Confectioneries

Role of Institution in the Promotion of Rural Women Entrepreneurs

Government recognized rural women as a source of potential entrepreneurs and have initiated many programmes to give financial, managerial, technical and marketing assistance. Various institutions and agencies were set up to give training and financial, marketing assistance to tiny, cottage and village industries.

1. State industrial development corporation
2. District Industrial centre provide assistance through self-employment for educated unemployed youth.

Rural Development Programmes

The main objectives of integrated rural development programmes is to increase the income generating power of the family who are below the poverty line to alleviate the poverty. 30 per cent women should be the beneficiaries in rural development programmes run by the government. The main rural development programmes are:

- Indira Mahila Yojana (IMY)
- Rastria Mahila Kosh (RMK)
- STEP
- NORAD programme

Indira Mahila Yojana (IMY)

Indira Mahila Yojana was launched in August 1995. Its main objective is to give a forward thrust too education, awareness, income generation capacity and the empowerment to women.

Rastriya Mahila Kosh (RMK)

RMK is also organizing training apprenticeship and orientation programmes, for trainers under Indian Mahila Block Societies (IMBS). The experience of RMK is that the women would have been able to double or triple their dairy income with the credit support of Rs. 2000/or Rs. 5000 the activities followed may be dairying, petty-shop keeping and investment of the agriculture operations.

STEP

Science and Technology Entrepreneurship Park was started in 1987 with the objective to provide training to rural women for increasing their production capacity and income generation. In this programme, they give training in the areas of traditional business like agriculture, milk, fisheries, handlooms, khadi, development etc.

2.5 lakhs women have been benefited by this programme since its inception. Maximum number of beneficiaries of milk-producing area. In 1996-97 (up to 31st December, 1996) this programme has an expenditure of 1.44 crores and number of beneficiary women are 2490.

NORAD Programme

NORAD stands for Norwegian Agency for International Development, NORAD was established in 1982-83 to help the educated and uneducated women financially in non traditional areas of business like electronics, computer programmings, manufacturing of watches, printing, readymade garments etc. 64200 women are benefited by NORAD programme. In 1996-97 (up to 31st December, 1996) it has an expenditure of 355.91 lakhs and beneficiary women are 6065.

Strategies for Development of Rural Women Entrepreneur

The following strategies may be taken the empowerment of women:

1. Educating girls and women;
2. Facilitating their involvement in economic activities through development of their entrepreneurial and income earning capabilities and access to credit;
3. Involving women in policy formulation and decision making;
4. Encouraging socio-cultural change by exploiting gender issues and promoting effective implementation of equal rights through legislation;
5. Women expect less formalities in setting up the units, easy and quick processing of assistance from the Government agencies;
6. They must aware of the various Government assistances especially for women.

Conclusion

The participation of women in the economic life of a country is necessary for national development. Now the growth of women entrepreneurship has become socio-economic significance in a country like India. By opening a large number of small industrial ventures women entrepreneurs can strengthen the industrial base, provide employment opportunities and achieve balanced growth. Thus, emerging economic force of women entrepreneurs can contribute a lot to industrial development of the country.

32

Women in Cooperative Sector—Twenty First Century Perspective and Approach

Dr. Samwel Kakuko Lopoyetum
Mr. A. Lourdu Arockiaraj

Introduction: An Overview

Women cooperative is an autonomous association of women united voluntarily to meet their common economic, social and cultural needs and aspirations through a jointly owned and democratically controlled cooperative enterprise. Women's role as an active worker, producer of goods and services has not been duly recognised by the man dominated society. In the sense of power and privileged with certain exceptions women have always been relegated to secondary position. The movement for women's empowerment gradually gained momentum, and as a result women in India were granted equality in all aspects of life along with men. Although, the constitution of India grants equal status to the women, they are not in the position, to uplift their life status because of illiteracy, poverty and social conventions. Even in the societies, which are called advanced in which the women are sole bread owners they are still living in the state of subjugation.

In the twenty first century, there is growing awareness among the women segment, even in the recent year's they have made notable mark by competing successfully with men despite their internal and external barriers including social, psychological, economic and political problems. This has been possible due to adoption of relevant education, political support and lobbying, inherent awakening, urbanisation, legal safeguards, social reforms etc., but the status of women in rural areas remains worst than urban area.

In the twenty-first century, the participation and involvement of women in cooperatives is gradually increasing in India.

Women in Cooperative Management and Administration

Cooperative management connotes an effective and efficient utilisation of resources for the successful achievement of the objectives and for the common need of entrepreneur members, in accordance with the commonly accepted cooperative principles.

The above said meaning of cooperative management is common to all kinds of cooperative institutions and basically cooperative management is mainly concerned with the principle of *'Democratic Control'*. Women should be encouraged to join in the management and administration of the cooperative affairs.

Women can play an important part in the management and working of cooperative societies by being elected representatives (Directors). They can participate in the decision-making process and formulate new programmes and policies. In addition to strengthening the existing programmes as elected members of Board of Directors. This will help in developing a new stream of professional leadership in the women cooperative sectors.

The management of cooperative organisation is mainly concerned with the Board of Directors elected by the general body. The Cooperative Societies Act of 1983 of Tamil Nadu paved way for one third of the Board members and should come from the weaker sections i.e., women. In the cooperative management, itself, there are a number of managerial functions existing. The management expert has identified five important functions such as planning, organising, staffing, directing and controlling. *The Board member are responsible authority to take correct decisions at all the functions and operational levels of management.* The role of women representative is very limited and not forthcoming. Women are co-opted in the management committee; some are duly elected and nominated. At present, the male dominated cooperative sector and the role of women board members, some to exhibit unfavourable scenario but the willingness and capability to take decision will help them to take the cooperative society in to the twenty first century. Not only as board members but full-fledged members of the community/ society and decision-makers. It is heartening to know that all levels of management i.e., strategic management, management control and operational management, is handled by women in the cooperative societies which are directly established by women themselves.

Normally, their vision in management of cooperative mainly concerned with the future development of the cooperative society as well as their status in the long-run. It is usually said that, women are very sincere in their activities, majority of the women board members and paid executives are more sincere than men. They are even very dedicated, at the same time fault may be as a result of the force from higher authority and male domination.

The inefficiency from the side of women are caused because of their "ignorance and illiteracy" of the subordinate's action regarding the business activities of cooperative sector. This shall remain to be moot question in the spheres of life in the twenty first century.

Women get confidence to control the affairs of cooperatives. Encouraging women's active participation would give an effective and efficient management and administration of the cooperative society in the new millennium.

Basic Business Activities under Women Cooperative Fold

Women are eligible to organise any type of cooperative society, subject to legal provisions of membership. They can form their own cooperative organisations exclusively with women membership. Most of the women cooperative in India have been either sponsored or assisted by the Central or State Social Welfare Boards. A majority of women cooperatives were thrift and credit cooperative societies, encouraging the women to save and provide them with credit on easy lending terms. The industrial cooperatives and weavers cooperatives are next to none. The industrial cooperatives which are run by the women mainly engaged in activities such as tailoring, knitting, preparation of papped, jam, pickles, making of masala powder, garment making, etc. Now-a-days, women contribute to about 80 per cent to dairy production and fish farming and share half of leading cottage industries. We shall discuss each of these cooperative organisations in the subsequent paragraphs.

In Maharashtra, one women cooperative society is running a canteen and library. Numerous organisations linked to women are run on cooperative basis in Madhya Pradesh. Some cooperative are running their own nursery schools and medial centres. The rural women cooperatives were involving themselves in the handcraft, sericulture, floriculture, horticulture, poultry, bee-keeping, seed bank, sheep keeping, cultivation of flowers and medicinal plants etc., such cooperatives have provided benefits to women as they get gainful employment and render services to the needy women sector.

The need to ensure active participation of women in the cooperative movement could be further highlighted and brought into the main stream of national life and national economy. Cooperative Institutions at all levels including those at base levels have the necessary infrastructure to take-up various promotional activities such as women and children welfare activities (childcare), family welfare, nutrition, general education, adult education etc., in addition to their economic activates. Infact, women are the main cause for sustainable milk production as well as dairy development in India.

Cooperatives have given women greater opportunities to participate in the economic affairs of the community. While stating the role of women in cooperatives the late Prime Minister Sri. Rajiv Gandhi said, *"involvement of women in cooperatives is a practical programme for raising the status of women in the society on a very large scale, especially in those echelons of our society where are help and assistance are needed more"*. Thus, the cooperative provides many varied opportunities for women participation. No doubt their standard of living would improve and their family income and quality of life would be enhanced. Women optimism is very much seem in the twenty-first century.

Table 32.1. Women in Cooperative Sector

(value Rs. In Million)

S. No.	Women cooperative	1998-99	1999-2000
1.	No. of Cooperatives	8006	8393
2.	Membership	828,586	842,327
3.	Of which SC Membership	3.0%	3.02%
4.	Share Capital	163.1	160.419
5.	Of which SC Membership	21.9%	20.56%
6.	Working Capital	1167.9	1160.386
7.	Business Turnover	922.0	884.17
8.	Value of Product Produced	108.1	113.45
9.	Value of Sales (Total)	403.6	429.13
	(a) Raw Materials	87.8	87.93
	(b) Finished Product	153.4	154.69
10.	Societies Incurred Profit	39.2%	37.42%
11.	Cost of Management	176.9	170.26

Source: Indian Cooperative Movement—A Profile (2001) National Resource Center of National Cooperative Union of India, New Delhi.

Table 32.1 represents the women's position in cooperative sector in India. It reveals the success story of women's participation. The number of women cooperatives in 1998-99 were 8,006 and it increased to 8,393 in 1999-2000. The concept of cooperation is reaching the weaker section of the community, and they have realised that, cooperatives alone can uplift them socially and economically. As already mentioned, women are basically weaker in economic aspects, and their share capital contribution indicated downward trend from Rs. 163.1 millions in 1998-99 to Rs. 160.42 in 1999-2000. Government participation and role is also cut-down, lack of which results in direct effect on the working capital position and caused major reduction in the financial flour in business turnover. The women societies, which made some profit also, reduced its profits by nearly 2 per cent. The reasons for the societies incurring losses are (i) lack of support and advice from government and other organisations, (ii) increasing trend on the cost of management and administration.

Table 32. 2. General Information about Women and Youth Status of Women Employment by SGSY and Other Schemes

S. No.	Indicators	1999-2000
1.	Women Benefit SGAY Scheme	58019
2.	National Old Age Pencion Prg. Benef	1426122
3.	National Family Benefit Scheme	29541
4.	Houses Constructed for Women	69170
5.	Employment Generated for Women (lac/day)	14582.38
6.	Employment Assured Scheme (EAS)	113609

Source: Indian Cooperative Movement—A Profile (2001) National Resource Center of National Cooperative, Union of India, New Delhi.

The general information about women and youth status through empowerment and employment by SGSY and other schemes introduced by the Government of India in 1999-2000 have indicated that, nearly 58,000 women got employment opportunities under SGSY scheme. Now a days, the old age homes are ensuring and mushrooming around the country, it is the symptoms of emergence of western culture. The old age women, who are living without any support from both son and daughter are eligible to National Old Age Pension Programme.

In 1999-2000, under this particular programme, 14,26,122 women got benefited and likewise 29,541 women were brought under national family benefit scheme. In India, women are neglected, lot of women population are not allowed to share the financial and economic benefits along with men counterparts. The equal opportunity and equal right to posses the fixed assets, with men are practically not possible in practice. The Government of India framed policies and initiated programmes for constructions of houses to women particularly for rural women and 691 women beneficiaries came under this scheme. Moreover, 14,582.83 women got benefits through Employment Generated for women scheme and 1,136.09 in Employment Assured Schemes.

Table 32.3. Women Empowerment

S. No.	Particulars	Number of Women
1.	Women in Gram Panchayat	6,55,629
2.	Gram Panchayat	37,523
3.	Women in Zila Parishad	3,161

Source: Indian Cooperative Movement—A Profile (2001) National Resource Center of National Cooperative, Union of India, New Delhi.

The concept of women empowerment is presently given much importance by the Indian politicians and other women organisations. The talks on 33 per cent reservation are going on. Similarly the Gram Panchayats are giving much emphasis on women. As per Balwanthra Mehta Committee which was concluded by the Govt. of India to analyse the implementation of new Panchayat Raj System, women were given reservation in the public administration and community leadership of the area. Never-the-less, there are 6,55,629 women representatives working at village panchayat level. It is good sign that the women talks are taking part in the reconstruction in the process of the modern India. So far 3,161 women are in Zila Parishad.

Though, the cooperative sector is functioning successfully, women's participation in this regard is almost insignificant. In man dominated world, women's development and participation in various sectors are insurmountable struggle. As far as cooperative sector is concerned, the women's role is inevitable in promoting their own societies growth and development. Table 32.4, reveals the full picture about the women's participation and involvement in cooperatives. The trend of each aspect such as turnover, membership working capital, number of societies shows increasing trend during the past ten years. The turn over was Rs. 283.1 million in 1989-90 and increased to Rs. 884.1 million in 1999-2000 (see Table 32.4). The societies should concentrate more on profitable operational functions and reduce costs in order to stabilise frequent fluctuations in the business turnover. The membership position improved and went up from 539-3 million in 89-90 to 842.3 million in 1999-2000. The process of education and awareness programmes about the benefits of cooperatives has directly influenced the women talks and advice to organize their own societies such as dairy cooperative societies. It resulted in the higher number of societies and large increase during the last ten years. The trend of working capital position, shows increasing trend but during the last three years under review, it indicated downward trend due to lack of efficiency and effectiveness in the management of the societies affairs.

The 2000 census of India reveals that women education in the country is showing on overall increasing trend. Kerala keep the first position in women education level. Goa takes the overall educational percentage in India. Here, Table 32.6 reveals the beneficiaries position of women education programme, but in 1999-2000, the number of women beneficiaries increased to 1,09,875. It is due to the process of awareness among the women regarding the importance and significant of education. Women have realised that education can uplift them into greater heights, socially and economically.

Contribution of Women in Cooperative Sector

Though, Indian cooperative movement is the largest cooperative movement in the world, in terms of size and membership, participation and involvement of women in cooperative affairs is limited in certain areas. Women are

Table 32.4. Growth and Progress of Women Cooperatives in India

	89-90	90-91	91-92	92-93	93-94	94-95	95-96	97-98	98-99	99-2000
Turnover	286.9	326.9	224.0	342.8	446.2	592.6	811.3	984.5	922.0	884.1
Membership	539.3	580.3	586.4	685.4	715.7	591.7	692.6	897.8	828.6	842.3
Working Capital	596.2	684.9	1053.3	1295.4	1406.1	1478.9	1408.1	2041.4	1167.9	1160.4
No. of Socys.	5478.0	5799.0	5772.0	6175.0	6866.0	7195.0	8171.0	8714.0	8006.0	8393.0

Source: Indian Cooperative Movement - A Profile (2001) National Resource Center of National Cooperative, Union of India, New Delhi.

Table 32.5. Progress of Women Education Programme

Activity/Year	91-92	92-93	93-94	94-95	95-96	96-97	97-98	98-99	99-2000
Women Education Programme	104643	126471	130355	102868	138165	1075781	109217	106207	109875

Source: Indian Cooperative Movement - A Profile (2001) National Resource Center of National Cooperative, Union of India, New Delhi.

facing many difficulties to participate in the decision-making affairs, of the society, therefore, they are not in the position to develop their professional leadership qualities. Let us examine a few co-operative sectors where women have strengthen their roots.

1. *Dairy Cooperatives*

Dairy is yet another important source of livelihood in rural community. It is more labour intensive than crop cultivation. India stands in the first place in the livestock production, women plays a vital role in rearing animals like cows, buffaloes, cats, dogs, sheep, goats etc. Dairying provides continuous employment opportunity to the rural women. Basically dairying is an indoor activity (zero grazing system). The rearing of milch and domestic animals so far, needs professional approach. Rural women are mainly attaching themselves to dairy farming and their encouragement on dairy production is frequently increasing every year. A number of dairy cooperatives have been set-up and managed by women in Gujarat, Maharashtra and Andhra Pradesh. Some field surveys noticed that, majority of women cooperatives which were formed by men are now going into liquidation, because of lack of efficient and effective management. Women's performance in dairy cooperatives have been revealed by the well-known success stories of their dairy cooperatives, cited as Anand Dairy cooperatives. It is the best example of women's involvement in the cooperative sector.

2. *Thrift and Credit Cooperative*

Women's participation in credit cooperative societies is of two types, i.e., they participate in the urban and village credit societies. They have also established their own banks with exclusive membership and women democratic management. Women teaching staff have formed cooperative credit societies in some of the girl's schools and colleges. In-fact, the first women's credit cooperative society was established in Punjab.

Tamil Nadu, is one of the states which has more number of women credit cooperative societies. This credit cooperative provides loans to their members, for farming, dairying, producing handicrafts etc., by which they would enhance their standard of living, both socially and economically. Besides, these societies undertaken some social activities such as medical check-up camps, students guidance, family welfare etc. The women's cooperatives provides various facilities for generating employment opportunities to the women folks for their sustainable development and gainful livelihood.

3. *Industrial and Non-credit Cooperative Societies*

Industrial cooperatives undertaking deals with manufacturing of cloths, toys, baskets and undertaking stitching of garments, uniforms, embroidery, painting, leather works, food articles like pickles, pappads, jams, masala powders etc. Under industrial cooperatives, formed by women, there are various kinds of societies which were formed such as women labour contract societies, chalk societies, weaning food societies, footwear societies, coir societies, multi purpose cooperative societies, liquid soap cooperative societies consumer cooperative etc. Some institutions have been imparting adequate traning and financial accessibility from IRDP, NABARD and KVIC (Khadi and Village Industrial Commission). Also, the management of these cooperative societies are purely undertaken by women representatives elected by the members of the cooperative society. The non-credit agriculture cooperative enterprises includes forestry societies, sericulture units, horticulture units, consumer cooperatives etc.

Problems and Constraints of Women in Cooperative Sector

Problems are numerous in the management of the affairs of the cooperative society. Women are not excluded in this respect. They are facing many problems and constraints in the normal management of cooperative affairs. Some of these constraints are:

1. *Social Constraints*

Social factors hinder the development of women in many ways. The society has the record of *chaining* various responsibilities to the women neck. The society restricts the women's in acquiring higher position and better performance.

In cooperatives, women faced many problems from various levels such as political interference, officials hindrances are severely affecting the development of the women in the cooperative sector. In rural areas, these problems are finding more intensity and severity. Rural community has not recognised the vital role the women's can play in cooperative development. The social rituals and customs are the main constraints for the direct participation and involvement of women in cooperative sectors.

2. *Illiteracy and Ignorance*

The lower rate of female literacy is one of the important factors, which prevents the participation of women in management of rural cooperatives. The illiterate women feel shy to join the cooperative organization. It is the major problem leading to conceptual misunderstanding improper perceptions about the cooperative systems. Due to illiteracy, rural women ignored their actual functions and diminishes their role in adopting modern and latest management techniques/methods.

3. *Financial Constrains and Problems of Inadequate Initial Capital Outlay*

The rural women are the poorest among poor in the current LPG's era. They only earn money for their regular needs, so that their savings out of the revenue is nearly zero. They are not in the position to contribute even to the share capital of the cooperative society. In rural community, women are nearly housemaid for their husband. Even though, there are various financial agencies for providing financial assistance to cooperatives, yet the official constraints and procedures create barriers to fund the projects proposals emanating from the women cooperative sector. There is a big problem of inadequate capital outlay in the women cooperative organisations.

4. *Limitations of Cooperative Societies Act and Laws*

The Cooperative Societies Act prevent women to join cooperatives. As per the rules and regulations the village cooperative societies their admits only the members (those) who have their own land. Whereas, the women do not possess any land in their name as a result they are not allowed to become cooperative members. Even though the constitution of India brings equal rights and opportunities to women, cooperative law fails to encourage the women's participation and involvement in cooperative affairs.

5. *Frequent Political Interference*

The present cooperative movement is actually in the grips of politics. The political interference may lead to discourage more participation of women's in the cooperative sector. But the political interference is the major problem and hurdle in countries such as India and Kenya, because of government sponsorship of the cooperative movement. The politicians disturbed the successful and efficient women's cooperative activities which are highly productive in nature, and this ultimately may discourage them to go forward in the emerging cooperative venture.

6. *Problem Related to Organizational Policy Decision-Making*

There is no specific policies regarding the formation of women's cooperative and their participation in the management of cooperative organizations. This may lead to greatly affect the future progress and growth of the women cooperative organizations. Framing the organizational policies is the crux of cooperative management. Women are emotional in nature, sometimes they may lead to taking wrong policies and decision-making in the cooperative organization. The viability of such societies are doubtful if the decision-making process is not streamlined in the twenty first century.

Suggestions for Enhancing Women's Participation in Cooperative Sector

(a) It is necessary to create congenial atmosphere in the cooperative movement itself so that, women feel encouraged to participate actively in the affairs of the cooperative society. It needs proper social awareness on the cooperative concept and functions of cooperative organisation. The government should conduct various awareness programmes.

(b) Decision-making is the most important function in any management organisation. Women directors should be given freedom to take decision regarding all business affairs and segments of the society. It may lead to an efficient functioning of the cooperative society in the twenty first century.

(c) Leadership Development Programmes (LDP) and Management Development Programme (MDP) should be conducted by the federal level organisations like District unions/State federation/ National federation. It would increase their capacity to lead the successful cooperative society in to the twenty first century.

(d) The reservation of women in the management body of the cooperative organisation as quoted in the cooperative legal system, Act and Laws should be strictly quoted and insisted upon strongly. It should give the courage, confidence, and inspiration to women community to participate in the affairs of cooperative sectors.

References

Boite Anuradha, (1987). *Women Employment and Rural Development,* New Delhi, Gian Publishing House.

C. Ragunadha Reddy (1986). *Changing Status of Educated Working Women,* New Delhi, B.R. Publishing Corporation.

ICA Statement to the Fourth World Conference on *Women, Cooperative Dialogue,* Vol. 4, No. 2, May-Sep. 1995, p. 9.

Coady, M. M. (1950). *The Social Significance of the Cooperative Management,* Antigonish, Extension Department, St. Francis Xavier University.

Cooperative Initiative Panel, (2002), *High Lights of the National Policy on Cooperative,* The Link, Anand.

ICA, (1995). *The Role of Cooperation in Social and Economic Development,* Bombay, Asia Publishing House.

Verhagen, K. (1984). *Cooperation for Survival,* Amstardam, Royal Tropical Institute.

Arun Biswas and Vijay Mahajan (1997). *Sustainable Banking with the Poor: A Case Study on Women's Thrift Cooperative System in Warangal and Karimnagar District of Andhra Pradesh,* Hyderabad Cooperative Development Foundation, 1-41.

Gupta, K.K. (1986). *Impact of Cooperations on Weaker Sections,* Bombay, National Federation of State Cooperative Banks Ltd., 1-177.

Lalitha, N. (1996). *Women's Empowerment through Cooperatives,* Social Welfare, 43 (6), 22-26.

Rohit Parihar, (1993). Punjab Women Lead in Cooperatives, The cooperator, 30 (II): 494.

Usha Rani, T. Chandra Reddy and Subramanyam Reddy (1992). *Impact of Milk Producers Women Cooperative Societies on Milk Production and Marketed Surplus of Milk in the Chittoor Milkshed Area,* Chittoor Indian Cooperative Review, 30 (2); 118-121.

Anni Phizaklea (March 10, 1999). *Empowering Women Workers in the Textiles and Clothing Industries—Reflection's and Prospects,* Indo-British Workshop on Empowerment of Women in Cotton Textiles Industries, Karaikudi.

Jaya Arunachalam (March 10, 1999). *Empowering Women in the Unorganized Cotton Textile Industry Sector,* Keynote Address at Indo-British Workshop on Empowerment of Women in Cotton Textiles Industries, Karaikudi.

Sunitha, W.G., Keller, A.G. (1993). *Involvement of Rural Women in Dairy Cooperative Societies in Haryana,* Indian Cooperative Review, 30 (4) April, 367-375.

Ujwala Hiremath, (May 1997). *Women in Grassroot Politics,* Social Welfare, 44 (2), 7-16.

Zakir Hussain, A.K. (June 1999). *An Innovation in Micro-credit—A Scheme for Women in Tamil Nadu,* The Cooperator, 39 (12), 507-508.

Ambrose Pinto (July-Sep 2001). *State and Property Rights for Women,* Women's Link, 7 (3), 26-29.

Archana Sinha, (September 1999). *Empowering Women for Food Security,* Social Welfare, 46(6).

Hashami, S., Schuler S. and Riley A.P. (1996). *Rural Credit Programmes and Women's Empowerment in Bangladesh,* World Development, 1414: 635-53.

Mishra, R.V. (1999). *Cooperative for Empowerment of People,* The Cooperator, 19(2): 195-197.

Ramanujam, K.N. (1995), *Women's Cooperatives and Economic Development,* Kurukshetra, 53(6): 11-14.

Ravichandran, K. (1995). *Women in Cooperatives,* Annual Magazine, Kannur Institute of Cooperative Management, 44.

Sekra, R.P. (1995). A New Dimensions in Women's Cooperative Banking, Kurukshetra, 30(2): 26-28.

Subburaj, B., Lopoyetum, S.K. and Karunakaran, R. (2001). *Members Perception on the Social Impact of Dairy Cooperative Societies in Dindigul District - A Survey,* Indian Cooperative Review, 39(1), 41-45.

Subburaj, B. Lopoyetum, S.K. and Karunakaran R. (2001). *Members Perception on the Social Impact of Dairy Cooperative Societies in Erode District—A Survey,* Cooperative Perspective, 36(4), 30-41.

Nakkiran, S. (2000). *A Study of Socio-economic Impact of Agricultural Credit Cooperative in Tamil Nadu,* Unpublished Draft Report, Chennai, Tamil Nadu Cooperative Union.

Surinder Kaur, (March 10, 1999). *Empowering Women Clothing Works in the West Midlands of Britain - The View from a Grassroot Organization,* Indo-British Workshop on Empowerment of Women in Cotton Textiles Industries in India, Karaikudi.

Tamil Nadu Corporation for Women Development 2002. Annual Report 2002, Project Implementation Centre, Dindigul District.

Informal Women Entrepreneurs in Rural India

Dr. S. Kannan
Dr. A. Padrakali

The informal sector is defined as those establishments employing less than 10 persons with or without power. International Labour Organisation defines informal enterprises as "enterprises with a small scale of operation, family ownership, labour intensive units, adaptive technology and operating in unregulated and competitive markets". System and National Accounts (1993) classified informal sector as (I) Household sector (ii) Unincorporated enterprises. The household sector comprise (a) informal own account enterprises that are single member or partnership units (b) informal enterprises employing household members and other employees. The important constituents of the informal sector are manufacturing, trade and services. In manufacturing, rural women engage in making handicrafts, toys, baskets, candles, sweets, pickles, papada. They rear cattle and sell milk. In trade, they undertake the sale of flowers, fish, greens vegetables, fruits, grocery, grass (fodder for cattle), firewood, neera and ice apple and the like.

As per census 1990, the females comprise 437.10 million when the total population was estimated to be 940.98 million people. Thus, women constitute 46.5 per cent of the total population. There are 126.48 million women work force representing 28.9 per cent of female population. Among the women population only 1,85,000 women are self-employed. The self-employed women account for 4.5 per cent of total self-employed in the country. Majority of them are engaged in the unorganized sectors like agriculture, agro-based industries, handicrafts, handlooms, and cotton-based industries.

The participation of women in entrepreneurship increased to 11.2 per cent of the total 2.64 million entrepreneurs in India during 1995-96. Ninety per cent (79.4 million) of women workers are in the rural areas as against only 10 per cent (8.6 million) were in urban areas. Only 2.5 million women workers are in the organized sector. Women entrepreneurs are often mentioned with reference to the organised sector. The informal selling milk, flowers pots, leaf articles, grass, firewood, pickles, sweets, vegetables/fruits, food products and the like are the micro level informal women entrepreneurs in rural areas.

Statement of the Problem

It is a misconception that women employment is of secondary nature and plays only a supportive role to the male income to the family. Women employment has always been relegated to a secondary status. But the role of rural women in enhancing the income of the family is much more higher than that of the male in the family. The present paper is an attempt to throw light on the significance of informal women entrepreneurs in generating income for their families.

Study Area and Sample Size

This paper is based on the empirical study conducted in the five villages around Tuticorin town. 180 rural women entrepreneurs were interviewed with the help of interview schedule. In the selected villages 4 types of informal entrepreneurs namely, flower vendors, vegetable vendors, food products vendors, and dairy products vendors and considered for the study. Altogether 180 entrepreneurs, comprising of 45 entrepreneurs in each type of selected entrepreneurships were selected and interviewed by following random sampling method:

Findings of the Study

- The study revealed the fact that women entrepreneurs depend upon the family background and support for involvement in entrepreneurship.
- The major reason for involvement in informal trade is the abject poverty in their families. It could be inferred that rural women involve in informal entrepreneurships, not because of their inherent drives to achieve something but to meet the financial needs of their families.
- In rural India, women turn to self-employment and entrepreneurship as a means of earning for livelihood. Women enter business to shoulder the financial needs of their families.
- The rural women entrepreneurs assume entrepreneurship in addition to the traditional domestic work. Thus, they assume dual role, caring the family vis-à-vis earning for the families. They work for long hours and are rewarded poorly in the families. The role of these entrepreneurs is not brought into light properly.

The study reveals the fact that the young entrepreneurs constitute 7 per cent.

- The larger proportion of entrepreneurs could be found in the age group of above 40 years. It could be observed that higher the age of entrepreneurs, higher will be the participation in entrepreneurship.
- Among the total entrepreneurs, young entrepreneurs prefer flower selling than the other type of entrepreneurship.
- Entrepreneurs in the higher age group constitute greater proportion in the vegetable vending, operating street hotels, and dairy products selling.
- It is perceived that young women have inhibitions in undertaking vegetable vending, food products vending and dairy products vending and hence the middle-

Table 33.1. Age of Women Entrepreneurs

Age	Flower Vendors		Vegetable Vendors		Food Products Vendors		Dairy Products		Total	
	No.	Per cent	No.	Per cent	No.	Per cent	No.	Per cent	No	Per cent
Up to 20	8	17	1	2	3	6	1	2	13	7
20-30	9	20	6	13	7	16	10	22	32	18
30-40	12	27	10	22	21	47	16	36	59	33
Above 40	16	36	28	63	14	31	18	40	76	42
Total	**45**	**100**	**45**	**100**	**45**	**100**	**45**	**100**	**180**	**100**

Source: Field Survey.

Table 33.2. Husband's Occupation

Occupation	Flower Vendors		Fruits/Vegetable Vendors		Food Products Vendors		Dairy Products Vendors		Total Entrepreneurs	
	No.	Per cent	No.	Per cent	No.	Per cent	No.	Per cent	No.	Per cent
Casual Workers	30	66	24	53	21	47	8	18	83	49
Farm Works	8	18	12	27	6	11	5	11	28	31
Petty Traders	3	7	2	4	5	13	18	40	28	11
Factory Workers	4	9	7	16	13	29	14	31	38	9
Total	**45**	**100**	**45**	**100**	**45**	**100**	**45**	**100**	**180**	**100**

Source: Field Survey.

aged entrepreneurs constitute lower proportion in all the entrepreneurships. At the age of 40 and above they undertake these trade without inhibitions.

- Table 33.2 describes the fact that 49 per cent of the women entrepreneurs; husbands are casual workers. Another 31 per cent of the husbands of women entrepreneurs work in farms. Most of the occupations of husbands of rural women entrepreneurs are seasonal.
- The husbands are often unemployed and remain unproductive. As they work in seasonal employment, they are not able to earn regular income for their family.
- Thus rural women entrepreneurs have to bear all the responsibilities of the families.

Economic and Socio Empowerment Details

Details	**Flower vending women entre-preneurs**	**Vegetable vending women entre-preneurs**	**Feed product vendors**	**Dairy products vendors**
Average size of the family	5	5	6	6
Literacy level	Middle school level	Primary school level	Middle school level	Primary school level
Average annual income from entrepreneurship	16,000	12,000	15,000	13,000
Average annual income of the household	24,000	22,500	20,000	19,500
Income spent on food consumption	85%	80%	82%	80%
Women entrepreneurs contribution to family income	67%	53%	75%	66%

Source: Field Survey.

The average size of the family of the rural women entrepreneurs is 5-6 members. Thus, it could be understood that the rural women entrepreneurs adopt medium size family.

- The literacy level of rural women entrepreneurs is found to be low. The highest literacy level among rural informal women entrepreneurs is middle school level.
- The proportionate share of the contribution of rural women entrepreneurs, to their annual family income is worked out to be in the range of 53 per cent to 75 per cent. The study unfolds the fact that though the rural women entrepreneurs with their marginal capital undertake trade on a micro level, they contribute a greater proportion of income to their families.

Conclusion

The role of informal rural entrepreneurs is not brought into light till recent years. It is often assumed that domestic labour is the major contribution of either rural or urban women besides formal employment in organised or unorganized sector. Patriarchal society do not recognise the economic role of women in Indian economy. The contribution of women to all the aspect of the domestic domain is by no means easy to measure. But the role of rural women in income generating entrepreneurship is much important as that of their involvement in domestic activities. Rural Women Entrepreneurship in India has to go a long way from merely dealing and selling traditional agro and domestic products. They must also involve themselves in modern small scale units. If these entrepreneurs are trained and provided with required capital, rural India could reduce the migration of people to urban areas.

References

Medha Dubhashi Vinze, "Women Entrepreneurs in India", Mital Publications, New Delhi, 1987.

N. Kamaraju Pantulu and C. Swarajualakshmi, Development of Women Entrepreneurship in India; Problems and Prospects, The Indian Journal of Commerce, No. 193 December 1997, pp. 295-301.

H.S. Anitha and A.S. Laxmisha, "Women Entrepreneurship in India, Southern Economist, Vol. 38, June 15, 1999, pp. 11-13.

Strategies and Constraints of Women Entrepreneurs in Rural India

Mrs. M. Malathy

Introduction

India is primarily rural in character about 74 per cent of the population live in villages. Women constitute almost half of the population of India. In the rural sector, 33 per cent of the males and 56 per cent of the females are in the rural sector is idle and unutilized. This is mainly due to existing traditional social customs that put men and women on different footings and they are confined to four walls of home, children and family rituals.

Constraints of Rural Women Entrepreneurship

Women suffer the most in our country. The basic problem of a woman entrepreneur stems from the fact that she is a female. Woman is first seen as a woman and then as an entrepreneur. They task of female entrepreneurship is full of challenges. They have to encounter public criticism, family prejudices and opposition and social constraints in the process of establishing themselves as independent entrepreneurs.

1. *Cultural Constraints*

A majority of women entrepreneurs do not like to be swayed by the expedient and uproot the cultural values. They

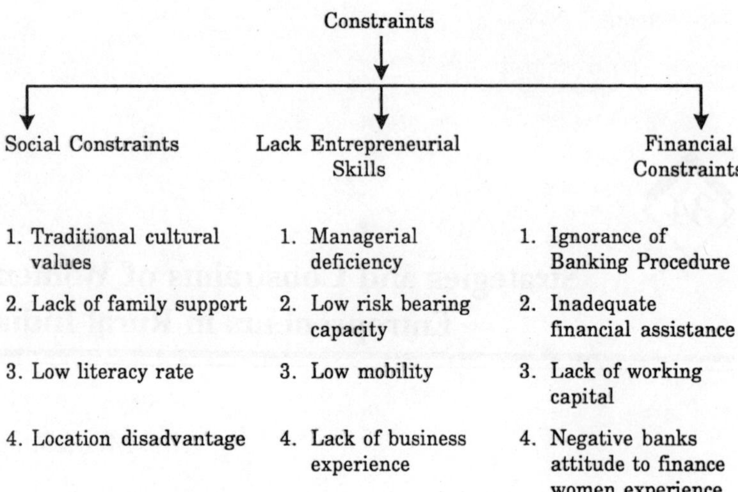

do not equate themselves with men but seek simply equal opportunities with them. They do not want to lose the basic fabric and thread of Indian culture for which India is known since the dawn of civilization.

2. ***Low Literacy Rate***

The low literacy rate among female is another serious hurdle. Female literacy rate is low as 30 per cent in rural areas as compared to 64 per cent in urban areas. Parents mostly in rural areas fail to see why their daughter must be educated as her training in household chores is considered more important. Another argument put forth is that educated girl would require educated husband and demand higher dowry. Parents find it more reasonable to spend on son's education rather than on daughter. Next reason is that mobility of girls tends to be restricted after attaining puberty and do not like to send to co-educational schools particularly in the middle and secondary level. To send girls to far off places for education is both economically impractical and socially unacceptable. Girls are expected to be married in their early teens to avoid social criticism. Moreover whatever the bookish knowledge she acquires in school colleges is not sufficient to meet the problem of the business world.

3. *Lack of Family Support*

Equal treatment of men and women is absent at the family level and social level. Social attitude are equally responsible for keeping women away from training and skill. In rural areas, the overbearing presence of elders restricts the young girls from venturing out and very strict boundaries are drawn around their mobility. The male superiority, ego, complex creates barriers in the path way of success. When she is upgraded in the business field, she has to face hostile reactions from her male colleagues. This situation is found even between husband and wife. Young unmarried women are discouraged to take up independent venture by their parents thinking that the venture will become property of her husband after marriage.

4. *Lack of Entrepreneurial Skills*

Rural Women Entrepreneurs are facing problems of managerial deficiency. Need for achievement, independence and autonomy are the basic ingredients required to an entrepreneur. Such requirements are either absent or found negligible quantities in a women. Risk bearing capacity is a crucial factor in running an enterprise is very low among women. They are easily disheartened by failure. Lack of information needed to achieve entrepreneurial success. Their shyness is considered as an ornament within the four walls of their home. This leads to poor communication ability and lack of self confidence lack of business experience and poor information scanning fail to tap market potential and encash opportunities provided by various Government schemes. The Enterprise taking second place to home. Women entrepreneurs have to make a fine balance between business and home. So time factor is a main critic. Lack of specialized training particularly in rural areas will hinder the progress of their business.

5. *Marketing Constraints*

Marketing is another very serious problem encountered by women entrepreneurs. Market competition has become very intensified due to introduction of a wide variety of product posing a serious threat to the survival of women entrepreneurs. Location disadvantage because of their rural background, they are not having accessibility to get enough orders and market exposure. They do not know how to market their produce. Establishing shops and showroom is the costly affair. Due to social environment prevalent, they are unable to move freely as quickly as an individual to move freely as quickly as an individual, to distant places to mobilize either resources or markets. Hence they are forced not to increase the production on large scale.

6. Financial Constraints

Although the problem of liquidity and finance are common to both men and women, it is acute for women entrepreneur. Rural women entrepreneur think that getting assistance from the government agencies is a lengthy process. Ignorance of banking procedure, lack of experience in formulating bankable projects are also the constraints of rural women. Very few women have property in their names. Banks have also taken a negative attitude while providing finance for women entrepreneurs that they can leave their business at any time.

In spite of so many hurdles and limitations, the participation of women in entrepreneurial activities are steadily increasing. Government recognised this particular section as a source of potential entrepreneurs and also as a special target group to development. Accordingly different developmental agencies have come up to assist them.

Strategies for Rural Women Entrepreneurship Development

1. Women must be motivated to come out of their traditional perceptions and responsibilities. There must psychological revolution in the society at large. Education is prerequisite to bring mental revolution to develop their personality. Firm determination hard work, and inter personal skills are strong points in promoting and managing their business.

2. Proper and specific need based field training by mobile training centre, part time training by mobile training centre, transport facilities, stipend can overcome their problems.

3. Government should provide timely and adequate

financial assistance and benefits such as loan, incentives, concessions, and subsidies to women need managerial, technical and counseling guidance.

4. Women expect less formalities in setting up the units, easy and quick processing of assistance from the government agencies.

5. They need market support and preferential treatment. This can be done by the government by taking over the product.

Conclusion

Women entrepreneurs have to face and overcome these obstacles to emerge as successful entrepreneurs. Further they will have to realize that entrepreneurs do not have a gender. Women entrepreneur in backward area needs special assistance and incentives from government and financial institutions by launching village adoption scheme through women entrepreneurial development programme. It is worthwhile to conclude by quoting the words of Pandit Jawaharlal Nehru. "When women moves forward, the family moves forward, the family moves, the village moves and the country moves up".

Social and Financial Constraints of Rural Women Entrepreneurs

Dr. S. Ganesan

Introduction

The people are familiar with the word 'entrepreneur'. But if asked to define it, the probability is that there would be as many definitions as the people to define. The term 'Entrepreneur' is of French origin, and its dictionary meaning is a person who organises and manages a business undertaking, assuming the risk for the sake of the profit.

A women entrepreneur is a person who is an enterprising individual with an eye for opportunities an vacanny vision, commercial acumen, with tremendous perseverance and above all the person who is willing to take risks with the unknown because of the adventurous spirit she possesses.

Women play a vital role in society. Her role is not restricted to the four walls of the household. She plays a role both at home and outside the home. This is true for both urban and rural women. In general, the women have the added responsibility of sharing non-household responsibility of earning. In rural areas farming is considered as a family enterprise in which women folk are equally responsible and contribute to almost all aspects of cultivator and other farm operations.

Though women is the key factor in the process of change and development, yet they are under-estimated in societies of most of the countries.

Focus of Women Entrepreneurs

1. Women constitute one-half of the segment of population in India. They can not be kept out of the mainstream of development.
2. Women are vital and productive workers in India's national economy. They make one-third of the labour force.
3. Enhancing women's economic productivity is an important strategy for improving the welfare of 60 million Indian households below the poverty line.
4. There is a significant gap between women's especially rural women's potential and actual productivity. The productivity gap of the poor women is much wider than that of poor men.
5. Indian women contribute a much larger share of their earning to basic family maintenance than men. Improving women's productivity income and quality of life, therefore, implies a multi-dimensional contribution to overall growth and development.

Basic Problems of Women

The basic problem or difficulty of a woman entrepreneur is that she is a woman. In this sense, she has to shoulder the twin responsibility of family and work. With joint family system, breaking up, many women simply don't have the support of elders. Women have been confronted by such dilemmas ever since they started leaving home for the work place. On the other hand, the attitude of society towards her and constraints in which she has to live and work are hostile. In spite of the constitutional equality and legal equality, in practice the attitude of men is not only tradition-bound but even of those who are responsible for decision-making, planning and research is not of equality. They still suffer from male reservations about a women's role and capacity.

This attitude of reservation creates difficulties and problems at all levels, that is, family support, training, banking, licensing and marketing. Women in rural areas have to suffer still further. They have to face not only resistance or reservation from men but also from elderly women who are ingrainted in the attitude of inequality.

In rural areas joint families are still the norm. The over bearing presence of elders restrain even young men from venturing out; so one can imagine how much a young girl needs to put up to become economically independent. Though in rural areas women are working along with men since times immemorial, their contribution in monetary terms remains unaccounted, or if at all accounted, it is given a very low value. They are mostly engaged in low-paid, back-breaking agricultural activities or act as helpers in handicrafts.

It is not that women do not have skills or capacity but they are properly trained or initiated in craftsmanship because it is felt that if a skill is imparted to a girl, it is wasted because when she gets married she takes away the skill with her. Therefore, a woman can only acts as a helper. She cannot function independently. Training and skill training is basic for any entrepreneurship. Facilities are available, many institutions are imparting training under various schemes but again social attitude keeps women away from them, both in urban and rural areas.

At the Government level, the licensing authorities and labour officers and sales tax inspectors ask all sorts of humiliating questions like what technical qualifications you have, how will you manage labourers, how will you manage both house and business, does your husband approve and the like.

The hurdles are not over as the biggest one comes now. And that is her marketing—both of raw material and of finished goods. To market her product she has to be at the mercy of middlemen who eat up a big chunk of profit. Here the middlemen try to exploit women entrepreneurs at both ends. They deny her discount or give the minimum discount in the purchase of raw material and on the other hand, try to extract maximum credit discount and commission on purchase of finished products from her.

If she decides to eliminate middlemen, it involves a lot of running about. Secondly, in these days of stiff competition, a lot of money is required for advertisement. If the product happens to be a consumer good, then it takes time to win people away from other products and make this product popular. And then the tendency is to always question, the quality of the product produced by women entrepreneurs, though many agree that women entrepreneurs are most sincere in maintaining the quality and time schedule.

Problems of Women Entrepreneurs

Need for achievement, independence and autonomy are the basic ingredients required in a successful entrepreneur, but these basic requirements are absent or found in negligible quantities in a women in India. She is held back by her own pre-conceived notions of her role in life. She sees herself only in the image of a product mother, wife and house-maker. She is proud to back in the glory of her husband, father, son and the like. This results in a conflict which inhibits achievement, independence and progress. Therefore, when the very urge is absent, how can she be motivated to be an entrepreneur?

All throughout her life-time she has led a protected life dominated by the family members. In her childhood, she relied on her parents or elder members of family, in her adulthood she relied on her husband and inlaws and gain in her old age, she depended on her husband and sons that is, at no time has she faced the risk of life all alone. Therefore, she has no confidence to bear the risk all alone. Then how can she be an entrepreneur, when business is nothing but a risk-bearing enterprise?

The overall literacy percentage among females is only 18.50 in India. A women is discouraged to learn more than the male members of the family. Due to this lack of education, she is unaware of technological knowledge, marketing knowledge and the like. Moreover, whatever the bookish knowledge she gathers is not sufficient to meet the various problems in the business field.

In India, it is almost only a women's duty to look after the children and other members of the family. Man plays a secondary or an insignificant role. Her involvement in family problems leaves very little energy and time to come out of her shell and play a significant role in economic development.

Equal treatment to men and women is absent at the family level and social level. When a women steps into the middle management or top management level, she has to face hostile reactions from her male colleagues, especially from those who are sub-ordinates or at par with her. The male superiority ego complex creates a barrier in the pathway of success. This situation is found sometimes even between a husband and wife and usually under such circumstance, a woman succumbs to male domineering ego.

The lack of information and experience makes it very difficult for her to select technology, market and location, and also to tackle problems related to labour and finance. The Government realising the need and importance of women entrepreneur's participation in the contribution to the economy have offered some assistance, thereby trying to create a favourable climate for women entrepreneurs to play a significant role in the rapid development of India.

As about half of all informal sector small enterprises world-wide are run by women, access to bank credit is vital for them, since few women have personal savings available for investment. At present, women are just marginally covered by the banking system. It has been estimated that only around 11 per cent of the total borrowings are by women in India. Many factors have been responsible for this inadequate utilisation of bank credit by women, example.

- Inadequate Size of Loans;
- Maring Money Requirement;
- Insistence on Collateral;
- Time taken to Process Loan;
- Tight Repayment Schedule;

- Ignorance of Banking Procedure due to Illiteracy;
- Lack of Experience in formulating bankable Projects;
- Lack of marketing, accounting and management skill leading to failure of projects and consequent inability to pay loans.

As a result of the above factors, small women entrepreneurs are frequently in debt to middlemen or money-lenders in India, who provide raw material or credit at extremely high rates of interest. To relieve these women from the vicious circle of indebtedness, exploitation and social disabilities and promoting self-employment amongst women, the nationalised banks and other financial institutions provide them credit at concessional terms.

Progress of Women Entrepreneurs

Progress of the women entrepreneurs in Madurai District as on 31.12.2002 are shown in Table 35.1.

Table 35.1. Progress of the Women Entrepreneurs in Madurai District

Sl. No.	Circles	No. of Groups	No. of Members	Savings (Rs. in lakhs)
1.	Madurai East	237	5656	52.24
2.	Madurai West	62	1160	4.18
3.	Melur	51	919	2.62
4.	Kottampatty	52	1000	4.33
5.	Thirumangalam	163	3656	75.15
6.	Kallikudi	66	1869	45.21
7.	T. Kallupatty	106	2359	41.64
8.	Vadipatty	288	6232	38.52
9.	Allanganallur	121	2209	10.69
10.	Tirupparankundram	145	2875	13.75
11.	Chellampatty	194	4219	43.04
12.	Sedapatty	204	4202	34.58
13.	Usilampatty	161	3212	32.40
	Total	**1850**	**39568**	**398.35**

Source: Office of the Planning Commission, Women Entrepreneur Corporation Limited, Madurai-2.

Various Scheme

Scheme of the Women Entrepreneurs in Madurai District as on 31.12.2002 are given in Table 35.2.

Table 35.2. Scheme of the Women Entrepreneurs in Madurai District

Scheme	No. of Groups/A/C	Amount (Rs. in lakhs)
SGSY/RF	535	135.00
EA	211	286.62
THADCO	3	3.26
NABARD	1154	1396.62
NGO	601	122.88
IFAD	795	785.39
Total	**3299**	**3329.79**

Source: Office of the Planning Commission, Women Entrepreneur Corporation Limited, Madurai-2.

SGSY - Sorna Jeyanthi Gramma Survey Rojgar Yojana

RF - Realving Fund

EA - Economic Activity

THADCO - Tamil Nadu Harijan Housing and Development Corporation

IFAD - International Funds for Agricultural Development

NGO - Non Gaztted Office.

Problems of the Women Entrepreneurs Surveyed

With a view to make indepth analysis of the problems of women entrepreneurs, a survey was conducted with the help of structured interview schedule by choosing 50 entrepreneurs by adopting convience sampling technique.

The sample women entrepreneurs were asked to rank the various problems faced by them. To understand the problems in the order of importance, Garret's Ranking Technique has been used.

$$\text{Garrett's Formula} \quad \frac{100\,(R_{ij}\text{-}0.5)}{N_j}$$

R_{ij} = Rank given for the item by the jth individual

N_j = Total ranks given by the jth individual.

Table 35.3 reveals that the problems of women entrepreneurs surveyed.

Table 35.3. Problem of the Women Entrepreneurs Surveyed

Sl. No.	Problems	Rank
1.	Inadequate Loan Amount	I
2.	Family Involvement	III
3.	Lack of Education	VI
4.	Male Dominated Society	V
5.	Tight Repayment Schedule	VIII
6.	Ignorance of Banking Procedure due to Illiteracy	IV
7.	Lack of Experience	VII
8.	Lack of Marketing	II

Source: Primary Data.

Table 35.3 shows that among the various problems faced by the women entrepreneurs in Madurai District, 'Inadequate Loan Amount' is the major constraint followed by 'Lack of Marketing', 'Family Involvement', 'Ignorance of Banking Procedure due to Illiteracy' and the like.

Conclusion

To-day, there is a greater awakening among women. Given an opportunity, they will deliver the results. In education, they have not only excelled but also become top makers. Like-wise, in office and industry, many have shown brilliant results. Even in rural India with education, women have shown better performance.

Educating women is absolutely essential in strengthening her personality. The need of the hour is to provide an opportunity is a conducive atmosphere, free from prejudice and vengeance. The need for awareness motivation to be an active member of the society and courage to correct the faults of men, are greater challenges of this decade. It is, therefore, encouragement to the growing intensity of motivation amongst educated young women for coming in the entrepreneurial stream and extend support with scientifically designed package of the technical and financial assistance.

The non-government organisations have a bigger role in stimulating and nurturing the spirit of entrepreneurship amongst women. Towards this end, an integrated approach is necessary for making the movement of women entrepreneurship a success. For this purpose, both the Government and non-government agencies have to play a vital role.

Chinnapillai of an illiterate old woman in Melur village was awarded with *Shakthi Puz Khar* award of Rs. 1,00,000 under the Social Empowerment of Women Entrepreneur. She has created 240 women entrepreneurs in and around Melur. The award was given to Chinnapillai by the Honourable Prime Minister of India, A.B. Vajapayee in appreciation of her service to the poor illiterate woman entrepreneur living in rural areas. In the present scenario, we want many Chinnapillais to create more *Women Entrepreneurs*.

References

1. C.B. Gupta and N.P. Srinivasan, *Entrepreneur Development,* Sultan Chand & Sons Company, New Delhi, 1995.
2. Vasant Desai, *Dynamics of Entrepreneurial Development and Management,* Himalaya Publishing House, Bombay, 1995.
3. District Industry and Commerce, Alagar Koil Road, Madurai-2.
4. Office of the Planning Commission, *Women Entrepreneur Corporation* Limited, Madurai-2.
5. Dawn Foundation, *Women Entrepreneur,* Arasaradi, Madurai-1.

Socio-psycho Constraints of Rural Women Entrepreneurs

Prof. C. Eugine Franco

Entrepreneurship

Entrepreneurship is the purposeful activity of an individual or a group of associated individuals undertaken to initiate, maintain or organise a profit-oriented business unit for the production and/or distribution of economic goods and services.

Emergence and Development of Entrepreneurship

The emergence and development of entrepreneurship is not a spontaneous one but a dependent phenomenon of economic, social, political, psychological factors often nomenclature as supporting conditions to entrepreneurial development. These conditions may have positive and negative influences on the emergence of entrepreneurship. Positive influences constitute facilitative and conducive condition for the emergence of entrepreneurship, whereas negative influences create inhibiting milieu to the emergence of entrepreneurship.

Women Entrepreneurship

Any woman or group of women who innovates, imitates or adopts an economic activity may be called women entrepreneurship. In India, women entrepreneur constitute a negligible proposition of the total entrepreneurs. There are more than 295680 entrepreneurs claiming 11.2 per cent of the total 2.64 million entrepreneurs in India during 1995-96. Attitudinal constraints, social traditions and kinship system inhibit the emergence of women entrepreneurs.

Rural Women Entrepreneurship

The phenomenon of women entrepreneurship is largely confined to metropolitan cities and big towns in India. However, women entrepreneurs are found in rural areas also. A rural woman entrepreneur is a woman or a group of women who undertake to organise and run an enterprise in a rural area. Rural women entrepreneurs face special problems and constraints. These are illiteracy, lack of education, lack of virtual information, lack of experience and training, low risk bearing capacity, limited mobility, feeling of insecurity etc. In addition, there are structural constraints in the form of inequality limited purchasing power, condemnation by local elite etc. They have also to face competition from the urban women entrepreneurs who make more attractive and cheaper products due to modern technology and large scale production.

Socio-psycho Constraints of Rural Women Entrepreneurs

India is a country of great traditions where social customs and norms exert a firm grip over the behavioural pattern of an individual. Although some women entrepreneurs have excelled in their enterprise, the fear of success arisen out of socio-psycho sphere system haunt women in general. The socio-psycho constraints impeding the growth of women entrepreneurship are as follows:

- Poor self-image of women
- Inadequate entrepreneurial motivation
- Lack of courage and self-confidence
- Inadequate encouragement
- Lack of social acceptance
- Afraid of failures and criticism
- Susceptible to negative attitudes

- Non-persistent attitude
- Lacking in leadership qualities
- Lack of ability in decision making
- Low level of social participation
- Discriminating treatment
- Lack of education
- Faulty socialization
- Role conflict
- Cultural values
- Unjust socio-economic system
- Lack of freedom of expression
- Lack of opportunities to acquire business skills
- Unfeasibility to work in project round the year
- Health problems
- Lack of emotional maturity
- Excessive tension and challenges.

Conclusion

Rural women entrepreneur have been on the business scene for several years and some have achieved remarkable success too. However, they are still not found in large numbers. Rural women need at this point of time, a coordinated support system to enter the mainstream of economic activities. On the other hand, rural women entrepreneurs are unable to make satisfactory progress because of sociological and psychological constraints.

Women Entrepreneurs—A New Trend in Rural India

Sivagami
Mrs. M. Pushpa
Ms. P. Sorubarani

Since independence development of women has been the centre-stage of development planning and 'welfare' oriented approach was adopted in the first four five year plans. In the V plan the approach was changed from that of 'welfare' to 'development'. The VI plan adopted a multi-disciplinary approach with three pronged thrust on health, education and employment. In the VIII plan there was a shift in the approach to women's development. It emphasized more on empowerment of women. Thus 'women empowerment' is the approach adopted by the government since the VIII plan. The year 2001 was celebrated as women's empowerment year. However empowerment of women is impossible unless she becomes an equal partner to men in social and economic life. Even though our constitution guarantees equal status to women as that of men in all respects, the real condition is not so.

Thus there arises a need for comprehensive and holistic policy on women, which would enable the country to fulfill the constitutional mandate of women's equality and objective of women's total involvement in national development.

Even though women constitute nearly 50 per cent of the total population, the percentage of women work force is only half of their population. Out of the total self-employed groups women constitute only 6 per cent to 8 per cent.

Thus the need for women entrepreneurs in the national development was felt and more emphasize was given to women empowerment since the VII Five-year Plan. The industrial policy resolution adopted in 1991 highlighted the necessity to provide special training programmes to develop women entrepreneurship. Promotion of women entrepreneurs requires a multipronged approach. Women should be motivated to come out of their traditional occupation and accept challenging and rewarding economic activities. The funding, promotional and regulating agencies should be motivated to be considerate and helpful towards women entrepreneurs.

Poverty Reduction Schemes for Rural Women

Till the early seventies, the main emphasis of the planned development was on the growth of the economy and overall development. But in the changed policy environment of the nineties, more emphasis was given to poverty reduction programmes for women.

Poverty reduction programmes for women in rural India have been conceived with the following strategies in mind:

(i) awareness generation initiatives;

(ii) promoting self-employment through credit and training;

(iii) providing lean season wage employment;

(iv) promoting savings habit among women;

(v) providing a range of support services to meet gender needs; and

(vi) addressing minimum needs such as nutrition, health, sanitation, housing and education.

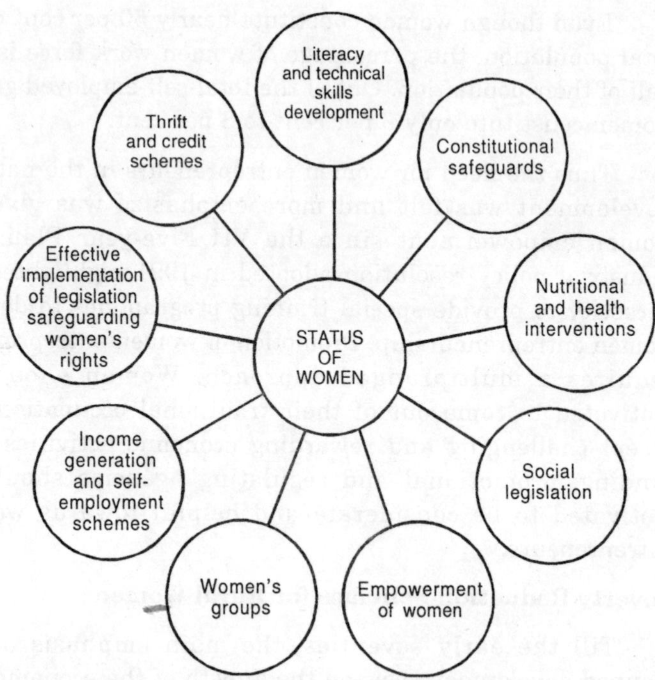

Institutions in Aid of Women Entrepreneurs

The entrepreneurs are born and can also be made. It is possible to identify the individuals with entrepreneurial talent, motivate and train them through properly organized programmes. Thus EDPs are very useful to harness the vast untapped human resources.

Several organizations are engaged in conducting entrepreneurship development programmes in India. The first step in this direction was taken by Small Industries Development Organization by setting up Small Industries Service Centres.

IFCI established Entrepreneurship Development Institute of India at Ahmedabad in 1983, for the creation of institutional infrastructure for entrepreneurship development. In the same year, the central government also established National Institute for Entrepreneurship and Small Business Development (NIESBUD) for co-ordinating the activities related to entrepreneurship and small business development.

Moreover, the government also established Rural Entrepreneurship Development Institute (RED) at Ranchi in 1983, Rural Management and Management Centres (RMEDC) at Maharashtra and Training cum Development Centres (RDCs) to increase interaction between entrepreneurs and enterprise.

In addition to the above institutions, commercial banks and financial institutions are also conducting entrepreneurship development programmes. A number of specialized institutions came up to provide training and entrepreneurship development programmes to various target groups—educated, unemployed persons, women, technicians, foremen physically handicapped and rural artisans etc.

The Centre of Entrepreneurship Development (CED)

This centre conducts entrepreneurship development programmes.

Small Industries Development Bank of India (SIDBI)

It conducts specially designed entrepreneurship development programmes to promote rural entrepreneurs.

National Aliance of Young Entrepreneurship (NAYE)

It is a pioneer in promotion and development of entrepreneurship among women. It started a women's wing in 1975. It organizes a number of national and international conferences for women entrepreneurs to make them self-reliant and increase them status in the society.

- Association of Women Entrepreneurship of Karnataka (AWAKE) and Self-Employed Women's Association (SWWA) are fighting for women's rights and striving to promote entrepreneurship among women.

Women Entrepreneurs Association of Maharashtra (WIMA)

It provides a forum for members and helps them to sell their products. It also conducts training programmes to women entrepreneurs.

Mahila Vikas Nidhi (MVN)

It was introduced by IDBI to provide aid to voluntary agencies in decentralized industries for training-cum-production centres and management and skill upgradation.

Support to Training and Employment Programmes for Women (STEP)

The programme of STEP launched in 1987, aims to upgrade the skills of poor and asset less women and provide employment in traditional sectors like agriculture, animal husbandry, dairy, fisheries, handlooms, handicraft and village industries.

Financial Institutions Supporting Women Entrepreneurs

Over the years, financial institutions and banks are playing a key role in providing finance and counselling to the entrepreneurs to start new ventures as well as modernize, diversify and rehabilate sick enterprises. Multifarious schemes such as Technical Scheme, Special Capital Scheme, Seed Capital Scheme, and Single Window Scheme are introduced to provide finance to entrepreneurs. Let us discuss some of the schemes introduced for the benefit of women entrepreneurs:

- **Mahila Udyam Nidhi (MUN):** This scheme was introduced by IDBI to help women entrepreneurs by providing equity assistance to new units;
- **Rashtriya Mahila Kosh (RMK):** It was set up in 92-93 with a major objective of meeting the credit needs of the poor women particularly in the informal sector;
- **Indira Mahila Yojana:** It is aimed to empower women through a sustained process of awareness generation and their direct access to resources in order to share and demand social and economic development;
- **Self-Help Group:** Illiteracy, poor health and social deprivation compound the limitations of the poor whose only asset is often their labour. To overcome

these limitations a novel strategy was developed and promoted by NABARD viz., Self Help Groups. Members of SHGs are identified through surveys or with a help of BPL list prepared by DRDAs in each district. Banks and NGOs interact with such people especially women to form small homogeneous groups. These small groups are encouraged to meet frequently and collect small thrift amounts from the members. They are taught simple accounting methods so that they maintain them own accounts.

Economic empowerment of women starts with savings and internal lending. But this does not take the rate of growth to sustainable level to raise the family income above poverty. So external credit linkage is necessary and it is obtained through the following schemes:

- Swarna Jayanti Gram Swarozgar Yojana (SGSY);
- Swarna Jayanti the Shahari Swarozgar Yojana (SJSRY);
- Tamil Nadu Adi Dravida Housing Development Corporation (TAHDCO);

The following case study exhibits the role played by Self Help Group in equipping the oppressed with socio-economic empowerment.

In Usilampatti, People's Bank has been formed by Dalit women for Dalit women. It was started in 1999, with an initial common fund of Rs. 1.12 lakhs, by collecting Rs. 50/- from each member a month. Now it has swelled to Rs. 4.30 lakhs.

The bank has sanctioned 118 loans to Dalit women, mostly farm workers, for housing, setting up shops, educational purposes and cattle rearing. The disbursal stands at a staggering Rs. 6.54 lakhs. The recovery is close to a healthy 75 per cent, which even many nationalized banks could not achieve.

Assistance for Marketing of Non-farm Products of Rural Women (MAHIMA)

Extending credit and credit linked promotional assistance to agencies dealing with marketing of non-farm products of rural women with a view to giving a fillip to their efforts for creating a "niche" or "pro-women" market.

Promotional Assistance will broadly cover activities such as:

- Initial market survey, feasibility/product study engaging marketing consultants;
- Capacity building;
- Quality control/testing equipment;
- Technology upgradation;
- Advertising;
- Branding/labelling;
- Packaging;
- Preparation of catalogues;
- Organization, participation in exhibitions/sales/fairs;
- Common marketing activities;
- Sales outlets, mobile vans;
- Training programmes on marketing;
- Orientation/business promotion, skill development;
- Data building/documentation;
- Any other promotional activity connected with marketing of products of rural women.

Awards

The National Bank had instituted in collaboration with the Institute of Marketing and Management (IMM, New Delhi), awards to encourage successful women entrepreneurs.

Conclusion

Thus women entrepreneurs in rural and backward regions need special assistance and incentives from the Government and other associate agencies. What is more, training of lakhs of women entrepreneurs in the coming decade is a yeoman task for various agencies.

Financial Problems of Rural Women Entrepreneurs

Vennila Fathima Rani, S.

Introduction

The word Entrepreneurs has been taken from the French language where it cradled and originally meant to designate an organised of musical or other entertainments.

An entrepreneur is one of the important segments of economic growth. Basically an entrepreneur is a person who is responsible for setting up a business or an enterprise. In fact he/she is the one who looks for high achievements. He/she can be defined as catalytic agent of change and works for the good of the people (Manickavel, 1996). According to Akhouri (1989), entrepreneurship in the economic field refers to identifying innovative ideas, product services, mobilizing resources and finally marketing them, covering the risk with constant striving for growth and excellence.

In the competitive world jobs are going to be limited, unemployment is on the rise hence there is need to took to other pastures. Self-employment opportunities and entrepreneurship is the most powerful tool to eradicate unemployment.

Women Entrepreneurs

Women entrepreneurs may be defined as a woman or

group of women who initiate, organise and run a business enterprise. In terms of schumpeterian concept of innovative entrepreneurs, women who innovate, initiate or adopt a business activity or called "women entrepreneurs. In nutshell women entrepreneurs are those women who think of a business enterprise, initiate it organise and combine the factors of production, operate the enterprise and undertake risks percentage handle economic uncertainty involved in running a business enterprise.

Status of Women Entrepreneurs in India

A large number of Indian women are slowly emerging out of a system that had oppressed and exploited them for centuries. Women are becoming self reliant in large numbers of cities, towns and rural areas. They are the vehicles of silent socio-economic revolution (Pant, 1997). According to 1991 census out of total 843 million people in India, females comprise 406 million representing 48.3 per cent of the total population. There are 99.4 million women workers (representing 28 per cent of the female population), but among them only 150,000 are self employed that accounts for only 5.2 per cent of the total self-employed people.

Majority of these women are engaged in the unorganized sectors like agriculture, agro based industries, handicrafts, handloom and cottage based industries. Participation of women as industrial entrepreneurs is comparatively a recent phenomenon commencing from 70's onwards.

Women Entrepreneurs and Finance

Although men as well as women face difficulties in establishing an enterprise, women have particular barriers to overcome. Among them are negatives prevailing socio-cultural attitudes, practical external barriers, and personal difficulties. Negative attitudes are frequently based upon sex discrimination, so called gender bias. In dealing with the various stakeholders associated with her company—such as suppliers, bankers, or customers—women often suffer from low credibility. Some men have negative perceptions of women as serious business people; these tend to consider women—run businesses as hobbies. Moreover, governmental laws and institutional policies that reflect this attitude sometimes hobble women. Not infrequently prospective women entrepreneurs in the western world have been humiliated when seeking business loans by being obliged to have their husband co-sign the note. Difficulties are made worse by such external barriers as lack of access to information and technical expertise or informal networks that exclude women but are important source of help and counsel for men. Because significant growth in the number of female entrepreneurs is a relatively recent phenomenon. Women have few role models and little opportunity for finding female mentors. One of the most difficult problems has been a lack of access to business loans from traditional banking sources. Women who want to start an enterprise often do not meet the conditions of commercial banks a positive history of borrowing, property to offer as collateral to secure a loan, and a business "track record". Further, the amount of money they want borrow is generally too small for banks to consider. An attitude among some male bank officials that women cannot handle money only adds to the difficult of obtaining needed finance even though many women often handle their family's financial matters and have proved themselves to be responsible and cautious borrowers. A few women had to resort to tapping costly credit through their credit cards. Government plays an essential role in fostering conditions for success. They can do this by creating a stable macro-economic environment, by reducing barriers such as arbitrary restrictions and a meddlesome bureaucracy, by providing the necessary infrastructure of reliable communications, transportation, energy and technology, and directly supporting creation of new enterprises.

We need a strategy that is multifaceted; a gender-specific set of strategies and a mainstream strategy. Government must first exert leadership, be a catalyst, a problem solver and a risk sharer. Next, we must identify potential partners in collaborative investment opportunities. These can include business mentors, mainstream investors, and financial intermediary organizations. Third, we must create and implement new interventions and financial products to elevate women's business investments into a comprehensive financial system. Last, we must employ the new telecommunication technology as a channel for matching investors and women business owners. Women leaders must engage in shaping public policy for the full spectrum and full continuum of financing, from the smallest to the largest business.

Financial Institutions in the Service of Women Entrepreneurs

The existing financial mechanism available in the country for providing financial support to women enterprises and small businesses needs careful scrutiny. It has been the experience that financial institutions in general have been dealing with women enterprises and small businesses in no better terms than their usual ways of providing assistance to the trade and industry (Kumar, 1992). Experience of financial institutions and assistance agencies reveal that a major cause of enterprise failure has been inadequate capabilities of the entrepreneurs to manage the enterprise (Gupta, 1990).

There are various governments and non-government agencies engaged in providing financial assistance to women entrepreneurs through various schemes such as Mahila Vikas Nidhi Scheme, Mahila Udhayam Nidhi Scheme, Industrial Development Scheme, Delhi Financial Scheme, Stree Shakti Package (SBI) etc.

Sources of Finance

Table 38.1 gives throws light on the sources from where the entrepreneurs managed finances for investment in their enterprises.

Of the total samples majority of the respondents had invested 100 per cent of their personal finance in their business. Very few entrepreneurs depended partially on financial assistances from banks and non-banking financial institutions revealing that women entrepreneurs are more likely torely on their personal finances for venturing into business.

Tabel 38.1. Various Sources of Finance Used by Women Entrepreneurs

Source of Finance	% of total amount invested						Total
	0	1-24	1-24	25-49	50-74	75-89	%
Self	5	3	5	8.5	23.6	55	100
Relatives	55	20	12	23.5	3.5	3.5	100
Banks	86	8	3	-	-	-	100
NBFI	88	7	2	2	-	-	100
Pvt. Financier	97	3	-	-	-	-	100

The data regarding percentage of capital expenditure reveals that the majority of the respondents (76.6 per cent) had not spent any money on procurement of land. This is supported by the data that the majority of the women entrepreneurs owned the premise for the enterprise. While (21.6 per cent) had spent amount ranging from 75 per cent and more on erection of the building quite a large percentage i.e. 48.3 of women entrepreneurs spent only 25-49 per cent of the capital on plant and machinery. This showed that the low investment in plant and machinery might be due to the involvement of cheap and simple technology. About 23.3 per cent of the respondents reported spending unto 24 per cent on procurement of raw material, publicity etc.

Status of Loan Repayment

Majority of the entrepreneurs (61 per cent) did not require any loan for launching business. Out of those who did require 68 per cent had successfully repaid the acquired amount. Thus showing that women entrepreneurs are prompt repayers of loan.

Reveals that influential contacts were ranked first followed by guarantee cover by the respondents in acquiring loan. Some of the respondents felt that due to lack of inheritance rights, property not in their names and lack of contacts it was difficult for them to provide guarantee cover.

The third most important factor reported by the respondents in acquiring the loan was feasibility report. The respondents felt difficulty in preparing report in spite of the fact that most of them were graduates.

Awareness about Special Financial Schemes

It reveals that 27 i.e. 45 per cent entrepreneurs knew that there were certain schemes for financial assistance to women entrepreneurs poor level of awareness of the women entrepreneurs. There is resulted to advertise and publicize these schemes to increase their level of awareness. Further analysis of the data revealed that only 5 per cent of the respondents had high level of awareness i.e. only 3 respondents could name more than 3 schemes large percentage of women entrepreneurs i.e. 65 had poor awareness i.e. they could only name of the schemes available for women entrepreneurs.

Problems Faced by Women Entrepreneurs

Table 38.2 indicates that the maximum number i.e. 23 (38.3 per cent) of the respondents said that that had little knowledge about procedures for making loan and they found difficulty in following the procedures. This is in rate of the fact that majority of the respondents were graduates. Many of the respondents (30 per cent) also reported that the financial institutes don't put much faith on them and sometimes of them with suspicion. Other problems expressed by the respondents were lack of funds, high rate of interest, non-implementation unexisting policies for financial assistance to women.

Table 38.2. Problems Faced by the Women Entrepreneurs

Problems faced by the women entrepreneurs	No. Respondents	Per cent
Lack of funds for initial investment	13	21.6
Lack of knowledge about procedure for taking loan	23	38.3
Non implementation of existing policies	14	23.3
High rate of interest	7	11.6
Women not taken seriously	18	30.0

Level of Satisfaction

Table 38.3 depicts the satisfaction level of the women entrepreneurs regarding adequacy, ease of securing timeline of finance.

Table 38.3. Level of Satisfaction of Women Entrepreneurs Regarding Finance

Characteristic	Level of Satisfaction			Total
	High	Moderate	Low	
Adequacy of finance	12 (20)	39 (65)	9 (15)	60 (100)
Ease of Securing Finance	8 (13.3)	23 (38.3)	29 (48.3)	60 (100)
Timeliness	9 (15)	27 (45)	24 (40)	60 (100)

Regarding the adequacy of the finance majority i.e. (65 per cent) entrepreneurs showed moderate level of satisfaction. For ease of securing finance 29 (48.3 per cent) entrepreneurs allowed low level of satisfaction. Many of the respondents reported that because of difficulty in getting finance from outside sources they tend to rely inter personal finance. Regarding timeless of finance 45 per cent and 40 per cent of the women entrepreneurs respectively had moderate and low levels of satisfaction.

Recommendations

It is important to deepen our understanding of women-owned businesses, particularly very small enterprise (financing arrangements for start-ups, personal savings, loans from relatives, bank loans, average loan size, percentage of successful loan of applications, percentage of failed loans, etc.). It is also important to assess the relevance effectiveness of "good practices". Are they "best practices"? Should they be disseminated so as to promote proven financial products and tools? The following approached might be considered by policy and decision-makers and adapted at national and local levels:

- Promote greater women business owners' equity by increasing women's assets through savings programmes, homeownership, etc.;
- Promote appropriate loan guarantee schemes;

- Make a credit pool available to women from the smallest to the largest business opportunity in a "secondary market" for small business loans; develop micro business financing programmes;
- Increase access to credit by promoting the development of intermediary organizations, intermediary structures between large pools of capital and very small borrowers (Grameen bank) which can deliver small amounts of money to entrepreneurs at reasonable cost;
- Increase women's business success by promoting counseling services to women business owners from start-up to development, and access to support networks for training, information, market development, as well as social protection (health insurance) and child care;
- Promote possible partnerships between government and NGOs, and private sector lending in order to make this market attractive.

Summary and Conclusions

Entrepreneurship is not confined to any particular stratum of society. Sex or race, there is no difference between men and women on the basis of personality recognition etc. However women taking to entrepreneurial career still constitute only a small percentage of total self employed population in the developing countries.

- Majority of them had low initial investment and working capital.
- Majority of respondents invested hundred per cent of their personal finance to start the venture.
- Those who had taken financial assistance had repaid their borrowed amount.
- Major problems faced by these women were lack of funds for initial investment, lack of knowledge for procedures for acquiring loans, non-implementation of existing policies etc.

REFERENCES

1. Choudhary, S. 1996. 'Women Enterprise Development in the Changing Global Context', Hindustan Publishing Corporation. New Delhi.
2. Gupta, P., 1992. Male and Female Small Scale Entrepreneurs of Delhi— A Study' M.Sc. Thesis, Lady Irwin College, New Delhi.
3. Kumar, H.P., 1996. 'Innovative Financing for Women Entrepreneurs and Small Business', Technical Paper International Women Entrepreneurs Meet and Conference - 1996, CWEI, New Delhi.

Emerging Issues of Women Entrepreneurs in India

Dr. S. Michael John Peter
V. Sarvanan

With the growing realization for entrepreneurship in the state of dragon of unemployment in the country, it is given more importance, and the stress and emphasis is now more upon women entrepreneurs as their contribution, participation and percentage is very low. India is a vast country with an estimated population of more than 1000 millions of which nearly half are women. Entrepreneurship amongst women in India is relatively a recent phenomenon. It has been rightly stated by Pandit Jawaharlal Nehru "In order to awaken the people it is the woman who have to be awakened. Once she is on move the family moves, the village moves and the nation moves". Since 1975, the international year of women, there has been a global concern for the emaancipation of women in India. Various programmes are being conducted in order to improve the status of women. But peripheral interest has been shown in developing a realistic and well designed plan and programme for promoting women entrepreneurs.

Who is Entrepreneur

An entrepreneur is a dynamic agent of change, who is instrumental in transforming physical, natural and human resources into value added products and services. The entrepreneurs to be successful the environment must be conducive and the individual must have an interest initiative and drive in grasping the essential facts.

About 50 per cent of total population constitutes women, but women workers constitute only 16 per cent of total population out this 16 per cent, 80 per cent remains engaged in unorganized sectors. Entrepreneurship among women is a recent phenomenon. Entrepreneurship calls for all those personal abilities and characteristics which could be developed in women folk.

Growth of Women Entrepreneurship in India

Women in traditional societies are still confined to four walls of home, children and family rituals. In a male chauvinist society, women are not treated on par with their make counter parts. They are victims of social discrimination and prejudices. Women are not taught to bring the best of them on par with wings of their better-halves. Such orientation and role prescriptions inhibit the development of self-confidence, innovativeness, achievement motivation, and risk-taking-ability which are essential for an entrepreneur's carrier.

In India, the positions of women have always been rather ambivalent one in our culture. On the one side, she was raised to the status of divinity and on the other side, she was exploited as somebody lower in status to men in every life style. However towards the end of the nineteenth century, it would be true to say that women have started coming out of their homes for education.

Till recently 28 per cent of female population was employed in unorganized sectors and were confined to activities such as weaving, garments, handicrafts and food processing. For women enterprises starting and operating a business involves considerable risk and difficulties because of societies belief that women are not as serious as men in managing business. Women are still considered to be inferior to men in India. In a situation characterize by deep rooted age, old sex discrimination, women have occupied a place much below men. But in recent years, the area of women entrepreneurship is being given increasing attention in terms of Government concern, research and new courses etc. However there has been a limited work done in the area of women entrepreneurship in India.

Against this backdrop, the paper makes a modest attempt to review the various issues pertaining to women entrepreneurships such as pre-requisites, motivational factors and traits of successful women entrepreneurs and constraints in development of women entrepreneurship in India.

Constraints in Women Entrepreneurship

The problem (or) difficulty of a woman entrepreneur is that she is a woman. Therefore, the attitudes of society towards her and the constraints in which she has to live and work creates difficulties and problems at all levels, i.e. family support, training, banking, licensing and marketing. Women still suffer from male reservation about their role and capacity.

In general, majority of women who entered the field of entrepreneurship admit that they face problems like managing workers, marketing recovery of dues, fear of loss in finance, social and personal life, preparation of project report, machine purchase procedure for getting infrastructural facilities, raw material procurement obtaining credit, arranging collaterals for starting industry, lack of training skills, collecting subsidies, seeking exemption from electricity duties sales tax, income tax etc., problems of brokers, persistent dependence on men folk for success in their endeavour, claiming price preference etc. Inborn traits of femininity such as shyness inhibitions debilitate her enterprising spirit. It leads to lack of confidence of her women are more cautious about the environment in which they have to work. They do not have access to information on as much as men have. Her unfitness for bribery, corruption, living and dining in the business world may not become her a good business.

The various problems faced by the women entrepreneurs be classified into five categories:

(*i*) ***Industrial Problems:*** The women entrepreneur faces many problems in industries such as lack of supply of raw materials for interrupted production, lack of sufficient stock of raw materials in period of short supply and anticipated price change, time consuming procedure of procurement of raw material, variations in the prices of raw materials at different places, lack of marketing experience, competition from established and larger units in the production line, delayed disposal of produce, difficulty in getting money from buyer after sale and lack of sufficient finished goods for smooth sale operation, efficient customer service.

(*ii*) ***Financial Problems:*** Limited working capital, constant need of finance, inadequate amount advanced through financing agencies, difficulty in justifying claim for finances, economic incredibility of women and lack of collateral security are the various financial problems faced by the women entrepreneurs.

Management and Technological Problems

The women entrepreneurs face the problem of inadequate incentives provided by the government, long and complicated procedures to avail institutional help, lot of formalities and paper work delays sanction, non-cooperative attitude of the employees, frequent visit to institution, personal or political influences needed to avail institutional help quickly, bribery in the agencies providing subsidies incentives/loans, target-oriented approaches and lack of promotional activities, limited of institution providing technical training, lack of effective communication between field functionaries and women entrepreneurs, lack of communication and co-ordination between different agencies, lack of media support to update the knowledge and skill, lack of opportunities to acquire business skill, harassment of officials, incompletion of documents and other formalities, lack of infrastructure facilities, insufficient staff to carry out the project successfully, non-availability of skilled workers and experienced workers because the unit after sufficient exposure.

Social and Psychological Problems

The various social and psychological problems faced by the women entrepreneurs are: lack a self-motivation, lack of motivation from family and society, conflicts due to dual responsibilities, non-co-operative attitude of husband and family members, no appreciation for independent decision, non-consistent to traditional norms, lack of recognition and appreciation in the family, male dominance, lack of social contacts and lack of confidence in women's ability.

General Problems

The general problems are: excessive burden of work and responsibility, health problems, lack of leisure time and other activities, poor risk taking ability, inadequate credit orientation, lack of emotional maturity.

Strategy for Development of Women Entrepreneurship

- Women have to be made compatible of both social and economical worlds and empower them towards self confidence and self reliance.
- To motivate women to come out of their traditional perceptions and responsibilities, some psychological and social changes have to be inculcated.
- Women have the need to put more efforts to change people attitude, to aspire women in the society at large, women have to be stimulated to take right kind of action at right time.
- The tendency of women portraying themselves as "Poorane" should be changed.
- When given independence and freedom liberally the dilemma and conflict of being left alone should have to be overcome by women.
- Successful women in the field of entrepreneurship have to help other women in starting and sustaining in their business wholeheartedly.
- To become a source of stimulation the women as well as the society are to be highly motivated.

Stimulation is partially a responsibility of organizations (Non-govt., Government) and partially women themselves.

- All women entrepreneurs should join together and form co-operative societies to see their industries run effectively.
- Literacy levels of women have to be enhanced and education of women should be made compulsory.
- Entrepreneurship education and training at all levels have to be introduced (from basic education to P.G. levels).
- Promotion of women entrepreneurship as an important and valued component has to be taken care of.
- Women entrepreneurship research and applications from time to time have to be documented.
- To attune the young minds to business enterprise, entrepreneurship education should be imparted in secondary.

Development of Women Entrepreneurship in India

- The Government policy-makers have to re-evaluate the strategies on women education and their entrepreneurial development and it should be planned and implemented.
- To support and supplement women entrepreneurship, it should be in the form of training skill upgradation, managerial skills, production and marketing along with development programmes like health and nutrition, women and child welfare etc.
- Women should be made aware of various credit facilities, financial incentives and subsidies.
- To make women entrepreneurship development sustainable, a constant re-enforcement is required.

- Though it is necessary to help them, to initiate their enterprise, a constant follow-up and liberal financial support should be ensured to enable them in functioning and smooth running of their enterprise.
- For effective sustainable development and technology transfer to women entrepreneurs, proper training based on scientific inputs, suitable product ideas, product identification, market survey, project formulation and necessary approvals from the government at the right time with less legal formalities, soft recovery rules are of utmost importance.
- To overcome the problem of procurement of raw-materials to women entrepreneurs and also the problem of brokers and middlemen and problems in marketing of products of women entrepreneurs, the Government has to give a helping hand.

Conclusion

Women have the potential and will to establish and manage enterprises of their own. What they need is encouragement and support from the family members, Govt., society, male counter party. With the right assistance from varied groups mentioned above, they can join the mainstream of national economy and thereby contribute to the economic programme.

Self Help Groups and Rural Women Entrepreneurship

M. Manimaran

Introduction

Women in the unorganized sectors are suffering in several ways. Their economic status is very low. They do not have access to crucial input like credit. Empowerment of women has therefore assumed importance. Organisation of the poor people is crucial for their upliftment.

Plight of Rural Women

The World Bank Report (1991) has observed that "women are central to success of poverty alleviation efforts in the short and medium as in the long run".

The goals of poverty reduction and empowerment of women can be effectively achieved if poor women could organise into groups for community participation as well as for assertion of their rights in various services related to their economic and social well being.

The effective management and development of women's resources, i.e. their abilities, interest, skills and other potentialities are of paramount importance for the mobilization and development of human resource. Yet, many women do not assert themselves owing to social inhibitions and disabilities.

As per the 1991 census, women's share, in the country's labour force was only 28.6 per cent. The female work participation rate registered an increase from 14.2 per cent in 1971 to 22.3 per cent in 1991.

Of the 51.98 million females (main workers) engaged in agricultural and allied activities, 45 per cent were employed as agricultural labourers compared to which only 21 per cent of males work as agricultural labourers. Women's access to land ownership is extremely limited. Because of the seasonal nature of work, they get only 90 to 100 days of regular employment in a year. There is also wage discrimination, as both the minimum and equal wages are denied to women in many areas.

Lack of entrepreneurial ability and marketable skills restricted women to the traditional sectors which did not yield enough income so as to enable them to cross the poverty line.

Formation of Self Help Groups

The SHG is an association of people belonging to similar socio-economic characteristic, residing in same locality.

The SHGs are voluntary associations of people formed to attain some common goals. These are groups which have similar social identity, heritage, caste or traditional occupations, and come together for a common cause and manage resources for the benefit of the group members.

The SHG is a group of rural poor who have volunteered to organise themselves into a group for eradication of poverty of the members. They agree to save regularly and convert their savings into a common fund. The members of the group agree to use this common fund and such other funds that they may receive as a group through a common management.

SHGs are presently promoted by governments, development banks and voluntary agencies, with focus on social and economic issues, mainly thrift and credit programmes. They are also taking up issues relating to rural industries and modernisation of agriculture.

Workings of SHGs

The SHGs usually generate a common fund out of small savings from persons of groups collected on a regular basis by curtailing unproductive expenditure, sometime, the internal savings generated are supplemented by external resources loaned/donated by voluntary agencies involved in promoting and strengthening the SHG.

Apart there, voluntary agency provide formal training through which the women entrepreneurs acquire practical skills for managing the small scale enterprises such as garment making, toys makings, fruit processing, handicrafts, etc. Though the intervention of micro credit, the women entrepreneurs has benefited many things and shifted even their lives from rural areas into semi-urban areas.

The voluntary agencies provide financial support to start micro enterprises and also suitable place for marketing the produces of women entrepreneurs. In order to activate, the system of rural marketing, the voluntary agencies, sometimes, may act as internal agency for selling the products produced by women entrepreneurs. The voluntary agencies insist the SHG members to undergo training for technology ungradation and to give up-to-date market information for creating awareness on the matters pertaining to price trend of commodities in the marketing system in rural areas, the SHG members may easily sell their products in the villages which paver the way for self sustainability among women entrepreneurs.

Findings of the Study

In order to understand the effective performances of the SHGs, a study has been conducted by selecting 5 SHGs operating from Bodinayaknaur. The interview schedule has been devised to collect data pertaining to the effectiveness of SHGs in the economic and social empowerment of women in the study area.

From the analysis it is found that the Self Help Groups are organized to manage their economic activities better and are gaining empowerment in directions, which are appropriate to their needs, interests and constraints. They gained confidence from an increase in their relative financial independence and security. The increase in the literacy skills of the SHG members in another indicator of empowerment some of them learned to sign, to read and write and could do simple arithmetic work. The animators and representatives and SHG members got trained for this work by the SHGs with the help of Mahalir Thittam officials.

Decision making is the ultimate level of empowerment and equality. It signifies that women have started taking control of their lives and situation through attending group meetings, public functions, involvement in income generating activities, joining other women in social causes. The collective and integrated activities of the SHGs are presumed to have helped them in sustaining their family economically, giving better education to their children, meeting financial crises in the family, meeting any crisis independently. The SHG members are sensitized in acquiring an attitude of protest against various abuses, knowledge about their rights, and other social issues.

Better communication skills is another indicator of empowerment of women. Most of the group members of SHGs at Bodinayakanur are attending the group meetings and Grama Sabha meetings regularly. This develops their ability to interact and communicate with each other. It is also observed that Mutram a monthly magazine projects the SHG activities of groups in Tamil Nadu, creates a journalistic medium for the interaction of women at the grassroot, and briefly explains the various schemes.

Conclusion

It is observed from the study that revolution is taking place in rural areas because of formation of many Self Help Groups in rural areas. It is further observed that the rural women are really empowered socially and economically after having become members of the Self Help Groups. Hence it is the duty of the government to assist the women in starting many more SHGs covering the all rural areas in the country.

Financial and Social Problems of Rural Women Entrepreneurs

K. Ramasamy

Introduction

The concept of entrepreneur was generated in the 19th century especially the women entrepreneurs. In earlier days women are confined within four walls of the house. Their main function was to do their household activities. But now-a-days women are going outside for job and also to start new ventures. This practice is prevailed in metropolitan cities, urban and semi-urban areas. But in case of rural areas, women normally don't engage in any of the job not for business activities. Because they are not recognised properly even though they have necessary qualifications.

The country can achieve its economic growth, when the women entrepreneurs are created in rural area. Whenever the women entrepreneurs are more in rural area, they can provide better employment opportunities to the public, as a result per capita income of the country will increase and also the standard of living of the people will increase. It will lead to overall economic growth.

There are large number of institutions which are established by the Government. For e.g.

National Research and Development Corporation

Department of Science and Technology

Entrepreneurship Development Institute of India

Small Industry Extension Training Institute.

These institutions provide training facilities, financial facilities and project facilities to entrepreneurs especially for women entrepreneurs. Even though these facilities are provided by the Government, the women entrepreneurs are not emerging upto an expected level. Because, there are some problems/constraints. In order to find out these problems, a small attempt has been made, not only to find out the problems but also to solve those problems.

Area of Study

The study is conducted in and around Bodinayakanur. Bodi is embraced by the mountains. It is on the Kerala border and the beautiful Bodimettu is a landmark that connects Kerala and Tamil Nadu Cardamom, tea and coffee are the main cultivation.

Methodology

The study is mainly based on the survey method. In Bodinayakanur, women entrepreneurs are emerging in various fields viz., tailoring, beauty parlour, job works (typing, xerox, etc), catering services. The data about the women entrepreneurs are not available in anywhere. Hence 40 women entrepreneurs relating to different business areas are selected and the data are collected during February 2003 with the help of interview schedule.

Financial Constraints

Finance is the life blood of any business. Without finance, organizing and running of business is impossible. Finance can be classified into two. Short-term finance, long-term finance. According to the nature of the business the entrepreneurs have to select any one of the finance. The finance can be borrowed from the financial institutions, local money-lenders, friends and relatives etc.

The respondent views are explained with the help of the following table:

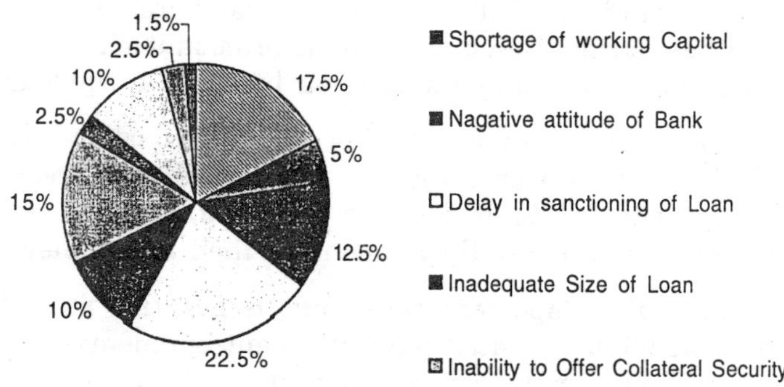

Table 41.1. Financial Constraints of Women Entrepreneurs

Constraints	Respondents
Shortage of Fixed Capital	7
Shortage of Working Capital	2
Negative Attitude of Banks	5
Delay in Sanctioning of Loan	9
Inadequate Size of Loan	4
Inability to Offer Collateral Security	6
Rigid Repayment Schedule	1
Ignorance of Banking Procedure	4
Bureaucracy and Red-tapism in Government Departments	1
Lack of Accounting Skills	1
Total	**40**

The data inferred from the above table indicate that the major constraints of woman entrepreneur is delay in sanctioning of loan, followed by shortage of fixed capital, inability to offer collateral securities, negative attitude of bank, ignorance of banking procedure and inadequate size of loan.

Delay in sanctioning of loan is the major constraints of women entrepreneurs. At the time of getting loan from the bank, the entrepreneurs have to submit the various records and they have to fulfill the various procedures. In order to fulfill these formalities, it will take huge amount of time. Hence the entrepreneurs cannot start their business at right time.

The second constraint is shortage of fixed capital. At the time of starting a business huge amount of capital is required. But it is very difficult to raise the capital by the women entrepreneurs because they depend on their family members.

The third important constraint is negative attitude of bank. The banker treated the women entrepreneur as mobile citizen. Whenever the women are married, they may move to their husband's place. Hence the repayment of loan will be difficult one to the women entrepreneurs.

The fourth important constraint is inability to offer collateral security. Whenever a person apply for loan, he has to provide collateral securities to the banker. This is not possible by the women entrepreneurs. Because the unmarried woman depend on her father and the married woman depend on her husband. As such as they don't have any of the properties in their own name to offer as collateral securities.

Some women entrepreneurs say that inadequate amount of loan is the major constraint. Some of the respondents say that ignorance of banking procedure in the major constraint.

Social Constraints

Apart from the financial constraints, there are certain social constraints which restricts the growth of women entrepreneurs.

The performance of the women entrepreneurs in case of social constraints are given in the table 41.2:

Table 41.2 revels that the major social constraints of women entrepreneurs are fear of social security (22.5 per cent). Normally the business people should ready to go to anywhere and at any time. This is possible by the men entrepreneurs. But most of the women entrepreneurs are not afford to travel very long distance out of fear on the night time without the support of male members.

Table 41.2. Social Constraints of Women Entrepreneurs

Constraints	Respondents	Percentage
Lack of Self-Confidence	0	0
Absence of Family Encouragement	3	7.5
Prejudice against Women	3	7.5
No Risk-bearing Capacity	3	7.5
Dual Role of Women	5	12.5
Male Domination	3	7.5
Lack of Exposure	2	5
Problems in Public Relations	8	20
Lack of Economic Freedom	4	10
Fear of Social Security	9	22.5
Total	**40**	**100**

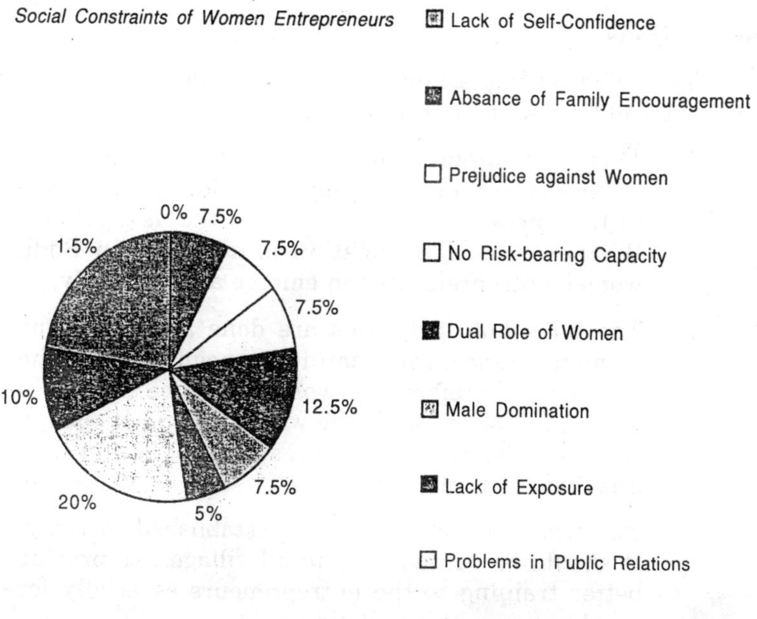

The second important constraint is lack of public relationship. As per the business, public relationship is vital to market their products. Women have good relationship with the women only in and around the house.

The third important constraint is due role of women. As the women are to perform the role of all the household works, they cannot concentrate in the business also.

7.5 per cent the women entrepreneurs say that the major problems are:

Absence of family encouragement

Prejudice against women

No risk bearing capacity

Male domination.

In my survey, lack of self confidence is 0 per cent. Each and everybody said that we have self confidence. Due to the absence of family encouragement and fear of social security, we cannot become a good entrepreneur.

Suggestions

The following suggestions are given in order to overcome the constraints of women entrepreneurs:

1. This is no organisation and association among the women entrepreneurs. Hence the Government have to take necessary steps to create the associations. Whenever good association is available in Bodi, women entrepreneurs can emerge automatically;

2. The household activities are done always by the women. Hence they cannot concentrate in the business. Therefore the work should be shared in between husband and wife which will given enough time for the women to engage in some form of economic activities;

3. The training institutions are established in cities. It should be spread over to all villages, to provide better training to the entrepreneurs especially for rural women entrepreneurs;

4. Most of the women entrepreneurs are unable to provide collateral securities. Hence they can form a group to start the business. This is one of the easiest way to provide collateral securities;

5. This group should conduct regular meeting to analyse the progress of the business;

6. The banking procedure should be simplified it should not be a lengthy process and the loan application form should be in regional language.

Conclusion

Our country belongs to rural areas. The development of the country is based on the develop of the rural areas. In order to develop the rural areas, more number of women entrepreneurs have to be created. Whenever more number of women entrepreneurs are there, they can provide good employment opportunities, as a result, the country will also be developed.

Women Entrepreneurs in Rural India

Nalini

The entrepreneur is a key to economic development. The emergence of women entrepreneurs in a society depends to a great extent on the economic, religious, cultural, social, psychological and other factors.

The women in India have been neglected a lot. They have not been actively involved in the mainstream of development even though they represent a bulk of the population and labour force. Primarily women are the means of survival of their families, but are generally unrecognized and undervalued being placed at the bottom of the pile.

Concept of Women Entrepreneurs

The Govt. of India can note women entrepreneurs as "an enterprise owned and controlled by a woman having a minimum financial interest of 51 per cent of the capital and giving at least 51 per cent of the employment generate in the enterprise to women".

Factors Influencing Women Entrepreneurship

1. *Pull Factors*

This factor encourages the women to become entrepreneurs that is it creates desire to do something new in life, need for independence, availability of finance etc.

2. *Push Factors*

This factors compel women to become entrepreneurs, they include financial difficulties, responsibility in the family, unfortunate family circumstances like death of the husband or father, divorce etc.

Types of Women Entrepreneurs

Dr. V.G. Patel, Ex-Director of Entrepreneurship Development Institute of India, Ahmedabad.

I. *Chance Entrepreneurs*

Start business without any preparation, clear goals or plans. They happen to grab the opportunities which they come across.

II. *Forced Entrepreneurs*

Start business due to some mishaps in their families like death of father or husband, divorce etc.

III. *Created Entrepreneurs*

Are properly identified, motivated, encouraged and developed through EDPs [Entrepreneurship Development Programmes] as a part to develop women as competent entrepreneurs.

Functions of Women Entrepreneurs

I. Imitation of successful entrepreneurs.

II. Introduction of new innovations.

III. Explore the prospects of commencing new projects.

IV. Take decision as to the nature and type of goods to be produced.

V. Managerial functions such as, formulation of production plan, arrangement of finance, purchase of raw materials, organizing the sales and personnel management.

Problems of Women Entrepreneurs

I. Lack of information needed to achieve entrepreneurial success.

II. Inefficient arrangements for marketing the products produced by women entrepreneurs.

III. They suffer from inadequate financial resources.

IV. Inferiority complex. They are easily disheartened by failure.

Industrial Network

(a) Development of entrepreneurship among women has received special attention of the policy makers.

(b) A special chapter in the 7th plan has covered the integration of women in economic development.

(c) The new Industrial policy has stressed the need for conducting special EDPs for women. Besides this, today a network of institution exist in the country to promote women entrepreneurship.

(d) Many organizations and associations promote and develop the women entrepreneurship by providing financial assistance at concessional rates of interest, conduct EDPs for women, create entrepreneurial awareness among them.

There is an acute need to reorient several things right from the grassroots i.e. increasing the number of vocational courses exclusively for women.

Women in background area (much be given) need special assistance from Govt. and financial assistance.

Thus the development of women as entrepreneurs will generate multifaceted socio-economic benefits to the country.